D1625009

ABU

DOWN ON THE BATTURE

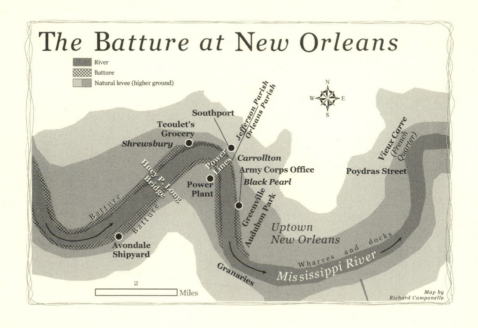

The Batture at New Orleans

- River
- Batture
- Natural levee (higher ground)

Southport
Teoulet's Grocery
Shrewsbury
Jefferson Parish
Orleans Parish
Vieux Carre (French Quarter)
Huey P. Long Bridge
Power Lines
Carrollton
Army Corps Office
Black Pearl
Poydras Street
Power Plant
Batture
Batture
Greenville
Audubon Park
Uptown New Orleans
Avondale Shipyard
Wharves and docks
Granaries
Mississippi River

2 Miles

Map by
Richard Campanella

Oliver A. Houck

DOWN ON THE
BATTURE

University Press of Mississippi

Jackson

www.upress.state.ms.us

The University Press of Mississippi is a member of
the Association of American University Presses.

Page 2: Mississippi River plantations, 1858. Adrien Persac, Norman's Chart of the
Lower Mississippi River (1858). Courtesy of Library of Congress.

Copyright © 2010 by University Press of Mississippi
All rights reserved
Manufactured in the United States of America

First printing 2010

∞

Library of Congress Cataloging-in-Publication Data

Houck, Oliver A.
Down on the batture / Oliver A. Houck.
p. cm.
Includes bibliographical references.
ISBN 978-1-60473-461-4 (cloth : alk. paper) 1. New Orleans Region (La.)—Social
life and customs. 2. Community life—Louisiana—New Orleans Region. 3. New
Orleans Region (La.)—Environmental conditions. 4. New Orleans Region (La.)—
Description and travel. 5. Houck, Oliver A.—Travel—Louisiana—New Orleans
Region. 6. New Orleans Region (La.)—Biography. 7. Mississippi River Region—
Social life and customs. 8. Mississippi River Region—Environmental conditions. 9.
Mississippi River Region—Description and travel. I. Title.
F379.N55H68 2010
976.3'35—dc22   2009043671

British Library Cataloging-in-Publication Data available

CONTENTS

DOWN ON THE BATTURE

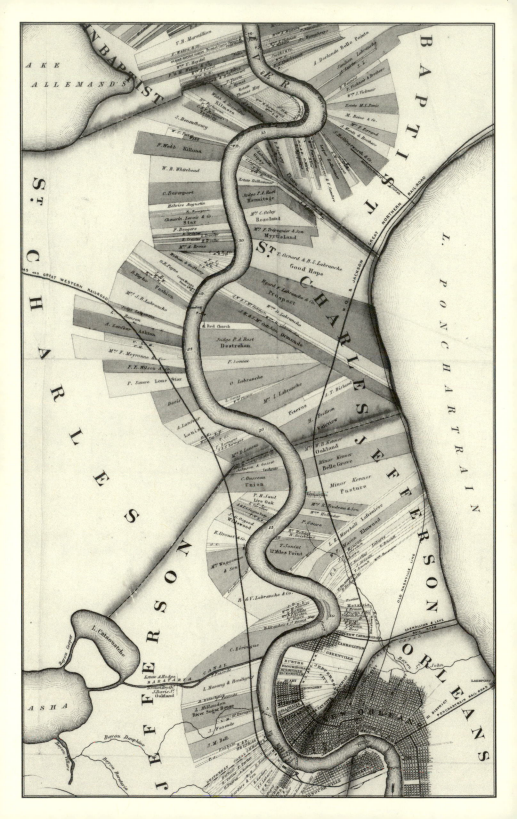

THE BATTURE

THE MISSISSIPPI RIVER winds past the City of New Orleans between enormous levees and a rim of land and trees. This is the batture, where the water beats against the land, and it is where the river breathes. At low water the batture may be a half mile wide, but come April it will often be zero feet wide as spring rains to the north swell the Mississippi from bank to bank, flooding the trees. It is one of the most surprising places in America.

The batture is largely woods here above the city, but it is certainly not wilderness. A scattering of construction yards and pumping stations give way upstream to grain elevators, power plants, and refineries. Against the banks rusty barges hold fast to their moorings. Out on the river, supertankers from world ports and tugboats the size of buildings are in motion, the drone of their motors more constant than the wind. Armies, gun boats, and entrepreneurs fought over the control of this traffic for three hundred years. Pristine is not the word that comes to mind.

It is, nonetheless, a wild place. Nobody manages the batture, not down in the trees. Its ownership and occupation are a tangle of obscure authorities, some as primitive as squatters' rights, and a briar patch for lawyers. Parish police monitor what they can see from their automobiles passing by on the levee top, and one levee board has gone a step further by posting NO TRESPASSING signs at the bottom, most of them contradicted by well-used trails that wind past them and into the trees. All of which help make the batture the rarest commodity to be found in an urban community, an undesignated space. It does not open at seven in the morning nor close at sundown, nor does it have rules about open containers. Or, setting aside guns and drugs, just about anything else.

One might think, horrors!—what an invitation to mayhem this is. Yet, I have frequented the batture for close to thirty years, often with a small dog in tow, and I have never been menaced, have never seen anyone more menacing than a bullying group of schoolkids one day who were quickly shamed as we came up and abandoned their pursuit. I have met all walk of people wandering through here, the majority of them on the short end of life, and my most frightening experience was finding a man I thought had frozen to death under a tarp on a morning that had caught sudden snow.

Here along the lower Mississippi, so close at hand, is a separate world. It has witnessed great ambitions, keelboats and steamers, expressways and casinos, glittering plantations, world-class pollution, and the severed heads of slaves on poles. It has also served as refuge for weekend fishermen, transients, teenagers, wild boars, and remarkable bursts of creativity, as we will soon see. It is a place where human beings come for the very purpose of being beyond the rules of designated places, to be in contact with the trees, the river, and a sky in the late day that is turning from light blue to pink to a violent orange, and a couple of men with cans of beer are looking at it, not talking a great deal, wired to a something that is vanishing before their eyes.

I take my dog and go down.

MOTORCYCLE

SOMETIMES I THINK I should have photographed the motorcycle, or nobody would believe me. I just assumed that it would last. So you'll have to take my word for it because there is no picture, only the wheels and a rotting log with a strange pan of concrete at one end. Who would know that it was the vagina?

The motorcycle sat apart from everything else in the woods. Squeezed between the river and the levee, this is the first stretch of trees upstream from New Orleans, past the docks and the stupendously plain buildings of the U.S. Army Corps of Engineers, lord of their domain, the largest structures on the levee until Vicksburg, and past the shell road from Cooter Brown's bar where the patrons come up on a warm night to drink under the stars without missing a beat of the music as it pours out the open door, and in the morning a condom on the grass. Then comes nearly a mile of trees and vines so tangled that either you follow the single path, down by the water, or you are in something like the Amazon, feeling your way. I would not have left the path this Sunday morning except for Ms. Bear, the dog. She does not do paths on Sunday and either I follow or I run the risk of losing her because the woods are full of rabbits and other interesting things that I can only imagine because, like all humans, I do not smell most of what the world has to offer.

You could not call it pretty in there. Off the footpath, which is really more a track used by occasional fishermen, you pick your way through the briars and over tree trunks felled by Hurricane Katrina. A tornado swept through half a year later, jumped the levee and then knifed down onto the nearby houses, removing the front of one so cleanly that its insides were exposed like a doll's house, the intimacies of our neighbors before our eyes. Before the storms, back in the heyday of the motorcycle, it was easier going through here. I just followed the sound of the dog ahead, listening for her sharp bark when she jumped a creature and then yelps of disappointment as she invariably lost it again, moving away from the river and towards the outside world. I could hear the sound of voices passing on the levee top, out in the full sun, animated phrases about who said what to whom at the office, in carpool, a different life out there which I was in here escaping for a while. Rounding the base of a big sycamore I saw the motorbike, gleaming.

At first I thought, what a strange place for someone to park a motorcycle. It was such a beautiful machine, painted bright green with its mirrors and motor in shining chrome, polished as if an hour ago. It was enough to retrigger my teenage fantasy, Marlon Brando in *The Wild One*, my certainty that with one of these sleek babies under me then Joanne Kylo, chief baton twirler for the Westfield High School marching band whose early developed breasts drew my gaze every school day for three straight years, would hop on to the seat behind me, wrap her arms around my waist and lean in against the wind.

I approached the motorcycle slowly, reverently, extending a hand out to touch it, when I noticed that there was an iguana coming out of the gas tank. More odd still, there were flowers sprouting from the pistons, and from the muffler the head of a snake. Even Ms. Bear had paused in her prowl to come near and give it a sniff, something quite different here. The iguana was made of rubber, the flowers were plastic, and I could only guess at the snake. We were in Disney World. That is when I noticed that the wheels were embedded up to the hubs in concrete. This sleek baby was going nowhere.

Then I saw the woman. She was lying on the ground next to the motorcycle. She was made of a huge log, entirely smooth, that dropped gently towards two rounded limbs. She had no head, but she did not need a head for gender identification because she had large breasts, up along the trunk, a pair of metal cones twirled in the fashion of a Tastee-Freez that perched on little concrete pans and were painted red and green. Their tips were covered with plastic tassels like favors from New Year's Eve. Mother Nature had cooperated even more actively with her legs, whose branches bent in natural curves and carried the feel of brand-new skin. Between the thighs, as they left the trunk, was the artist's most daring act, a spread of concrete tousled like hair and bordered by a rim of lips. Andy Warhol . . . Madonna . . . this was found art, exaggerated, in-your-face, and modern art, and it was deep in these woods where nobody in the world except someone following his dog who was following a rabbit would ever see.

I never met anyone else in that spot on the batture, and I went back many times. Once I took Lisa, my wife, and although she shared my sense of surprise the scene itself seemed to offend her. It was the woman, I am sure, although whether if it had been a man lying there instead with a large concrete penis her reaction would have been different I cannot say. I can't say either whether the motorcycle and the woman were connected, or had even been done by the same artist, but everything about them said so. Maybe they were the story of my adolescence after all. You get the motorcycle, particularly one this impressive, and you get the woman, particularly this one so impressively endowed. I think the artist's greatest stroke was to leave her face to the imagination, which allowed you to fill in your own fantasy, the face you dreamed of but never even kissed.

I asked Ricky once about the sculpture. He lives in these woods from time to time and knows what's what. Apparently Ricky hated the guy who did it, had a fight with him, he said. I could not make much more sense out of that because Ricky was not completely sober at the time, but it had something to do with a happening on the other side of the levee. All I can say for certain is that the artist was a guy, and he did not live in the woods, and he did not come back to hang out. I suppose that I could track him down, but it seemed a little like tracking down Bigfoot. Say that I found him, then what? We do not need to know everything in this world. There are times to treat mystery like wildness and leave it alone.

You could go back today and find the motorbike if you wanted. The sycamore tree is still standing, but the hackberry and willow are down all around and the new growth is a perfect mess. It is good for berries in the spring; they get lots of sun. Good for poison ivy as well, whose fresh leaves shine like wax plates and seem to drip before your eyes. There are many more rabbits than before, too, but as my dog could tell you they get away quickly and have more places to hide. The frame of the motorcycle still stands in its concrete well, but its adornments are long gone. No one comes and polishes it like it used to be, that is for sure. The woman has gone, too, pretty much. Her trunk has all but decomposed and her breasts have disappeared. What remains is a strange patch of concrete at the base in the shape of a triangle. That's about it. I visit it from time to time like a Mayan temple.

Years ago I read a story in the *New Yorker* about an artist visiting a coastal resort. He had flown in to hear Pablo Picasso speak, only the event was sold out and the hotel was crowded, so late that afternoon he found himself wandering the beach alone. It was a gray day, a cool mist falling, and the beach was entirely deserted except for an old man down the way who seemed to be playing at the edge of low tide. As he approached the old man, our visitor stopped to watch. The man was bent over and with a seashell he was drawing vigorous arcs on the wet sand flats, arcs that merged into a huge and enormously sad face with two mouths and three eyes, all on one side of its head. The man was short, muscular, and bald and there was no mistaking him—he was Picasso. The visitor stood transfixed, as if seeing God, as the man finished, tossed his shell into the sea, and walked away towards the hotel.

We were left with the visitor, the drawing, and the tide coming in. As we are with the motorcycle. Only, the Mississippi rises but once a year so it will take a little more time.

PROPERTY

THE BOY IS COMING STRAIGHT TOWARDS ME on the levee path, pedaling like a bandit, eyes wide, but I have no sense that he sees me. I am already stepping to the side to make way when he turns abruptly and plummets pell-mell down the concrete apron towards a fifteen-foot mountain of dirt at the base of the levee. His bike bucks with the impact and then surges up a path beaten into the side of the hill, tops the crest, and soars into thin air, rearing back in space like a rodeo horse, disappearing on the far slope. I hear a jolting crash, and then he reappears, circling out on the flats, his face in a victorious grin. "Yeah!" yell a couple of his friends on the levee top, one of them already gliding his bicycle away down the path to turn, get momentum, and make his run. It is beautiful and dangerous and exactly what kids do.

It will not last long here. Every spring as the high waters recede, somebody sends out a bulldozer which works over the flats near the power lines, blading and scraping the accumulated sediment into a large pile. Over the next several weeks dump trucks will come and take the dirt away. The hill will diminish. The dirt bikes will move on. The wild grasses will grow back. By fall they will turn into cover in which you can lose a small dog.

Nothing seems harmed, but I am struck by the anomaly that if the authorities are worried about the strength of their levee at this critical bend of the river, they are letting some good protection go. Less than a quarter mile upstream someone is paying someone a lot of money to moor barges loaded with heavy rocks against the batture, to buffer it against the action of the current. Which leads me to wonder whose dirt this is. For a long time this was the most crucial question in Louisiana. If you mention the word "batture" to a New Orleans native, if you look the word up in the library, you will find but one meaning: a flaming lawsuit that chartered the future of the waterfront for the most important port city of its time.

The Mississippi River batture is unique. Here we have a place that is neither water nor land; it is both. It depends on the time of year. Spanish and French traditions going back to the time of Rome recognized public rights to public things. The civil code declared that rivers and their banks were public, which would have closed the matter. But in the late 1700s along came a New Yorker with an American notion of private property, a keen legal mind, a nose for money, and an ambition as big as the Ritz. He would claim the batture. His brother would claim the river. Together, they would run the entire show.

Edward Livingston was about as close to genius as a Louisianan has come, at least one in public life. He was an accidental Louisianan, fleeing the North under several clouds including his support for the notorious Aaron Burr against Thomas Jefferson, and a serious money scam. He remade himself, adding a second marriage to a nineteen-year-old belle whose beauty is said to have been no impediment to his career. Livingston's accomplishments in the courthouse and the legislature remain monuments today, but the case that made him famous was about silt on the banks of the Mississippi. The silt was no different in any way from the dirt accumulating under the power lines by Ochsner Hospital where the bicycles now play, except that this dirt was at a prime location, at the foot of Poydras Street in downtown New Orleans. Livingston and his client who claimed the dirt stood to make a fortune. Indeed, Livingston declined a fee in the case. Instead, if he won he would get a piece of the victory, the most valuable real estate in New Orleans.

The American notion of property was not popular in New Orleans, whose people were accustomed to using the banks of rivers to beach their boats, promenade, fish, swim, rake mussels, and even take fill for their front yards. By precedent rising from centuries, the Mississippi batture was common ground. In a city oppressed by heat and the septic odors of life before sanitation, the batture was also treasured ground, the place where everyone in society from cotton brokers and their wives to boat hands and slaves could enjoy the breeze, air pleasant to inhale, and the very sight of the river. When Livingston's client undertook to develop the batture he was claiming, a public mob arrived to interrupt his work. Every day.

Livingston's client made a frontal assault. He went out at low water, diked off the batture, and then arrested people coming to take the river sand in the old and accustomed way. The ensuing lawsuits rivaled the twists and turns of a Dickens novel. On one side was Livingston, claiming that private property was sacred in America. On the other was a who's who of wellborn local names, Poydras among them, right on up to the president of the United States. Thomas Jefferson considered the public character of the Mississippi to be a civic right and essential to his ambitions for settling the West. After Livingston won his first case, Jefferson had U.S. marshals evict him from the batture anyway, at which point Livingston sued the officer who evicted him. It got that bad.

When the dust settled, years later, Livingston emerged with his property deed, but he had ceded important claims to the city, including part of his real estate and development controls on the rest. Compromise that it was, the New Orleans batture would go from small wharves and open space to an impressive accumulation of mega-wharves and warehouses. New Orleans not only could no longer access the river; they could no longer even see it. Except upstream, where nobody had seen fit to develop the batture and where there were only the levees and trees.

Enter Robert Livingston, Edward's brother, with an even more impressive list of accomplishments and a yet bigger coup in mind. He and Robert Fulton, who had either invented the steamboat or made a quick copy of someone else's, depending on your source,

tendered an offer to New Orleans that it could not refuse, a monopoly on the Mississippi River.

Fulton's steamboat had one huge advantage for the future of the
city; it could go upriver. The early flatboats didn't even try. They
made spring voyages downriver from as far away as Pennsylvania
and Ohio, sold their cargos at the foot of Canal Street, sold off the
rafts as well, and spent the rest of the summer getting back home.
Fulton's new boat, now resting in New Orleans, could get back up
in a week, although he had not exactly done it yet. The Fulton-
Livingston team proposed a deal. They would deliver steamboat
commerce to New Orleans, if the city would grant them all rights
to the river trade. They would own the river.

Enter another challenger. Henry Shreve came from the Red
River in northwestern Louisiana and saw Livingston's monopoly
as a threat to the future of his region. He built his own steam-
ship, sailed it down to New Orleans, loaded it with goods, and
sailed back home again to a hero's welcome. People did that sort of
thing back then. Fulton had only talked about going back upriver.
Now Shreve had actually done it, and with merchandise on board.
More threatening, Shreve tried it again. Livingston had to make his
move, and so, as the second Shreve boat was ready to leave New
Orleans with its cargo, he had the captain and the boat arrested.
The public sided against the Livingstons, as it had on the batture
cases earlier, causing a small riot. Shreve was released the next day.
A few months later a local judge dismissed the lawsuit. Edward
Livingston might own a piece of the batture, but Robert would not
own the river.

Two hundred years later, who owns the batture dirt is still not
crystal clear. Nor is who controls what is built on top of the dirt,
which is suffused by federal servitudes, parish levee rights, and con-
flicting private deeds. Out near Lake Pontchartrain, the Corps of
Engineers has cut down trees twenty yards back from the levees,
on the notion that a hurricane could knock one down, breach the
wall, and drown the city. Some day they may apply the same thinking to the batture woods. Or another Edward Livingston might

come along and start building condominiums on the batture, like the high-rises lining the beaches of Florida. Suddenly, this place seems precarious.

HIGH WATER

At high water we rediscover the river. For one thing, it is hard to miss the superstructures of the big ships passing along the skyline like pieces of scenery gone mad. We begin to check the river gauge readings in the *Times-Picayune*, how many more feet until flood stage. Like hurricane season, it is a worrisome force. There is another river, however, with its own cast of characters, which I find quite by accident while taking a bike trip up to Luling this spring when the Mississippi is rising to the foot of the levee and people have come out in force to meet it.

My first encounter is with James, at his usual high-water post opposite Ochsner Hospital under the power lines. He has three rods in the water and a catfish already on the bank. I first met James on an evening years ago. It was near dark, he had caught a big one and was loving it to shore. The fish was too heavy to raise up by the hook, so James slipped into the water and slid his arm around its body, big as a calf, cooing to it, calming it down. He moved his hand slowly up into the gills, all the while singing its death song, until he had the creature by the throat and could drag it out of the water like a log. Lord knows how he got it home.

Up past the Huey Long bridge there are scattered families from River Ridge with baby carriages and tricycles, nothing out of the ordinary for a beautiful day. As I near Rivertown, however, the banks explode into a jazz fest of family groups, coolers and chairs, the grill firing up on the levee top, radios blasting; it is a party. Down below, a line of fishing poles attacks the water like the opening day of trout season in Montana. Old men help young boys bait their hooks and cast out towards the trees. I see two hundred faces in half a mile, not a one unhappy.

Crossing the St. Charles Parish line, a sand and gravel operation blocks the river for nearly a mile, but farther on people are back in force. One couple is fishing in tandem. She is standing with the pole at the water's edge while he, trapped above in a wheelchair, makes arm motions showing her how to cast. His face is urgent. Of all the fishing I see today, this is the one I most hope lands a whale.

By St. Rose the river comes right into the levee again, and five boys are down in the shallows, lashing some large logs together in a raft. As I pass by them the tallest one hops onto the contraption, which rocks precariously, settles down, and he is afloat. Whether he later tells his parents about it I've no idea, but I'm not sure that Huck Finn told Aunt Polly either. The water is calm here and only knee deep, so I am not worried about them. There are certain things that boys have to do around water, and making a raft is one of them.

To the north, two grain elevators rise from the levee, which solves the mystery of the whistling ducks. Right after Hurricane Katrina, big flights of these dapper birds started pouring into Audubon Park, their excited cries filling the air. You started to hear them in the early evening from anywhere near the river, ragged lines overhead, going home. Only they had left Audubon some weeks ago and I could not figure out where home now was. Home, this Sunday anyway, is along the batture by the grain elevators, hundreds of whistling ducks, swimming and hanging out.

It is apparent why they are up here by the granaries. The are eating the spilled seeds, which carry chemicals in amounts that, while small, build up to killing levels in soft organs of the body. Pesticides managed to eliminate the brown pelican from Louisiana, two separate times. The whistling ducks are drawn to these elevators like geese to a baited field. What happens later to them and to us is all one big experiment with chemicals down here, and we will not know the results for years to come, perhaps generations. The Louisiana Chemical Association has declared that linking cancer rates along the river to toxic discharges is like relating miscarriages to people who "screw too much." The analogy has always eluded me.

I turn at the Ormond Plantation, stop the bike, and pull out some peanuts from the little pack under the seat. Off to my right, on the grass rim of the levee top, is a man of indeterminate age with skin that has clearly seen a great deal of the out-of-doors, reading a book. It is a hardcover book and it holds his attention completely. Next to him lies a dachshund, the color of mahogany in the late-day light. They are the only creatures in view. I think, there are probably a dozen places this man could choose to read a book, and most of them more comfortable, but here he is by the Mississippi River. And for the same reason I am. In the magic.

On the way back now, past the jubilee at Rivertown, the families are leaving, carrying their gear and, for the lucky ones, a fish over the shoulder. The place was looking pretty well trashed on the way out. As I ride by this time, with a big moon rising, two women are bagging it all up, the plastic jugs, beer cans, and food wrappers, and I wave and say, "Good for you, ladies!" You should see the Tulane campus after a party, or Elysian Fields following a parade. The women have a catfish on the bank, waiting. I would no more fry up a catfish from the Mississippi than I would one from Chernobyl. Here we have the largest river in the country, loaded daily with toxins, and a zone at its mouth the size of New Jersey so contaiminated there are no creatures living in it at all.

It would not take rocket science to clean up the Mississippi. Granted, a lot of our pollution comes from cornfields and hog farms upstream, but I have never heard a Louisiana official raise a peep in protest. The heavy metals and carcinogens, though, come out the discharge pipes of some 130 industrial plants crowding the batture between Baton Rouge and New Orleans. The state doesn't say much to them either. I once asked James about eating the fish he caught. He said, "Why not, we drink the water don't we?" I nodded my head, a lot of us do.

It is full dark now, the river banks are empty, and the high water is just a noise against the levee, rushing by. The families that were out here are home cooking dinner. Every few years the state issues a report on cancer rates, but the report is carefully general and does not identify the hot spots. The state will not disclose them, it says, for reasons of privacy. Exactly whose privacy, one wonders.

The people at risk are invisible for most of the year. They come out like a special species at high water. When the river goes down again, they will disappear from view.

SUPERBOWL

FIRST OF ALL, when they called me about a show on the Mississippi River I had no idea they meant at the Superdome. They said they were from *Good Morning America*. They wanted a local story to go with the big game. They talked about doing it from the French Quarter, but I said it would be better to film from the batture, maybe at Audubon Park. You'd be right at the river's edge, I said, you could reach out and touch the hulls of the big ships going by. They said ok. Then they told me the time in the morning. It was much too early. I can barely open my mouth before dawn. So I gave them the name of a colleague to call.

Back in the 1980s when this took place there were not many critics of the way the Mississippi River was being managed, and we were generally dismissed as kooks. New data was showing that the river levees had cut off the coast, which was sinking fast. Big canals were destroying the southern parishes, leaving the city of New Orleans naked to the sea. We sounded like the nerds at the company picnic who keep predicting rain. At least it was nice that a national network would cover the story.

The next day, a Saturday, they called back. My colleague was out of town. I have the flu, I said. You were out coaching soccer, they said. They had apparently talked with my wife. My cards were slipping away. We would film it next week when they got into town.

Midweek, they called again. They didn't have the stretch to go film on the river, they said, and besides the weather prediction was for rain. Why didn't I come down to their studio in the Superdome and we'd film it there. They had some footage of the marsh. We set Friday. They called back and reset for Saturday. They called back once more and reset for Sunday, game day. They would send a limo for me at 4:00 in the morning. When I told Lisa, she laughed.

And so on Superbowl morning, feeling nervous as a player, I am sliding into a black van large enough to carry a SWAT team and we drift noiselessly downtown. There is not a car on the road at that hour. The Goodyear blimp is hovering against a night of stars. I am led from the limo by a man in an orange jumpsuit who announces my arrival by walkie-talkie as we move up ramps choked with vans and cables, past the team locker rooms, and out onto the playing field. They have a photograph of the coast, orange jumpsuit tells me. I will look at it and say things like "big stakes," "one quarter of America's seafood," and "losing forty square miles a year." Then they will drive me home.

The stadium is immense and dark with a feel of the Spaceship Enterprise. Tiny humans are gathered on a platform at the near end under tall lights and reflectors. Makeup technicians are working on the faces of a man in a red sweater and a woman in bright yellow. I surmise that they are Mr. and Ms. Good Morning. They look carved from wood and are saying absolutely nothing to each other. I can see more human bodies sprawled about on dollies, coils of cables, and seats in the stands like the victims of a gas attack. Some are wearing band uniforms. Beyond them the dome disappears towards infinity, revealing only the outlines of a papier-mâché Statue of Liberty and a cardboard Mardi Gras crown.

Suddenly it is 6:00 a.m., the lights go up and Mr. and Ms. Good Morning burst into smiles. "Good morning, America," she says brightly. "It's a beautiful morning here in New Orleans," he asserts. They are both looking at TV monitors showing a picture taken by the Goodyear blimp outside and relayed to New York by satellite. All we can see around us is the black vault of the stadium. It could be snowing out there for all we know.

Immediately, Mr. and Mrs. Good Morning are off the air. I can tell because they have stopped smiling at each other. New York must be running an ad. Orange jumpsuit comes over to brief me. They will not have time to run the photo of the wetlands, he says. Instead, we will walk out on the Astroturf and, flanked by the Statue of Liberty and the Mardi Gras crown, I will talk about the river and the coast. It will take exactly forty-five seconds. I begin revising my lines. There is no coffee, anywhere.

They were not running an ad in New York. There had been a plane crash on Long Island and the studio had located a neighbor who heard it. Our presentation may be delayed. Above me in the stands the Olympia Brass Band is struggling to its feet. They look as if they slept here all night long. They stumble onto the field for a rehearsal, led by a man who is wielding an umbrella, but it is hard work there in the empty dome and the music disappears into the air. The band sits back down again. The tuba players fold over their instruments like pillows on a bed.

Just then, out from the players' ramp, comes a squadron of men in sweat suits. Could it be the Denver Broncos? The Forty Niners? They look a little overweight. It is the grounds crew. Jogging, hustling like high school tryouts, they untape a plastic tarp covering the field and roll it up. Nobody trusts the dome roof, apparently, even when it is not raining. They sprint off again, tarp in tow, not to be seen again. Why their exercise had to be performed at 6:25 a.m. and with such dispatch is one of the morning's unsolved mysteries.

At 6:30 a.m. I am on call again. First up in the next segment of the program. I am going over my lines. Should I talk about tons of sediment or migratory waterfowl? Mr. and Ms. Good Morning are back under the lights, looking my way, and just then a strange entourage emerges from the runway. Several large men in shirtsleeves are hustling a bearded giant towards us who must go three hundred pounds. Someone was caught gate crashing, I think. But then, why would they put that on television? Orangesuit comes over to share the news. "We've scored big time," he tells me. It is an injured player from one of the teams.

The lights go back up on the platform. Someone has provided plastic flowers and they are shining brightly. Someone has also

provided a couch, and there they are in a row, Mr. Red and Ms.
Yellow on each end, the injured giant in the middle. The conversation is fast and furious. Although the sentences are lost in the dead
air, I can pick up phrases like "champion" and "heart." This is a key
segment, at least four full minutes. Some sponsor is paying serious
air time.

As the lights go dim and the player is helped from the stage, orangesuit is back with more news. "I think we're next," he says, "but
we've only got twenty five seconds." So we won't walk anywhere.
Instead I'll just stand there on the plastic grass with the empty
dome behind. I begin scratching out the sediment numbers. It'll be
fish and birds I decide.

But no, it is the Olympia Brass Band's turn. A cardboard king
cake has arrived on a little cart and they are going to play "When
the Saints Go Marching In" and escort it around the field. Just as
they get to the cart, however, they are arrested by a man wearing
headphones and a bright nylon windbreaker. New York has located
some sports experts, he says. They need to discuss the implications
of the injury on the game.

The band retreats with its instruments without a word. I am
hoping they are paid by the hour, better yet, by the minute. My fate
is easier. Orangesuit comes over to say that the Mississippi River
story has been squeezed out. It's ok, I say. I ask about a ride home.
He is sorry about that, too. The limo is booked, taking the injured
player to his hotel. They'll call me a taxi. Send them the bill.

I draw a good taxi driver, an old one, slow on the accelerator,
slow on the turns. It is still early morning, and we are stuck coming
down Broadway behind a garbage truck, young men leaping off
to load the trash bags. "Those people do a day's work," I say. "Always was," says the driver. In the old days the garbage wagons were
drawn by mule, he adds, and they'd throw the garbage on, food and
all. "That's how they'd feed the hogs," he said. "Eat the food that fell
off."

I wondered aloud whether that made more sense than flushing
it into the river, as we do these days.

"But there was bad stuff in that food," the driver continued. "A lot of folks got the ptomaine."

"Didn't ptomaine hurt the pigs?" I said.

"Pigs got no veins," he said. "No way for the blood to get back to the heart."

I am torn between the vision of the hogs eating garbage and the Superdome. I am trying to decide which scene is worse, but it's really not a close call. Down here at the foot of Carrollton the sun is burning fiercely off of the levee grass, and it is going to be a nice day.

SPILLWAY

"Do you believe in jesusoursavior?" he asks me, first thing. He is holding a jar with a fish in it, but his mind is on the larger question. I'd probably not answer the question, but he cannot be more than six years old, and a small six at that. His buddies haven't come up to the top of the levee. They are still kicking around in the reeds below.

I am lying out on the grass along the spillway with my head propped against the bicycle seat, munching on a snack bar, which buys me a little time to answer. I say a little cautiously that I believe that Jesus was a very good man. This is clearly insufficient. "My mama says that if you believe in Jesus then you go to heaven." I think that this is actually a question, too, so I say many, many people believe that so she is probably right.

He still looks worried, though. He says, "Do you believe that boys can go to hell . . . if they've done a sin in the Bible?" I am the wrong person to ask here because what I really believe is that fears like hell can haunt a boy so badly that he wets his bed for years and learns to sleep with the light on, and I am talking from personal experience here, so this is one idea I am not ready to confirm. Instead, I ask him what he has in the jar, although we can both see perfectly well what it is. It is something living up in a pond on the spillway that leads from the Mississippi River to Lake Pontchartrain, guarded by huge gates that can be opened at flood time to reduce the head on the main river. Fortunately, however, the gates leak year round just enough to supply fresh water to ponds between. He tells me, "It's a fish," but his heart isn't in it. The hell idea has got him.

I offer him some M&M's and ask who his friends are. He says they are Joey and I didn't get the others, one of whom turns out to be his brother, because he comes up now and cuffs the little one and says, "We got to go home." My companion gets up to leave, looking hesitantly at the minnow which is wiggling around the muddy water in his jar. I give the fish five minutes in the house, maximum, before it is down the toilet. I say, why don't you put the fish back in the pond? I might as well have said something untoward about Jesus because he backs off without a word, clutching his jar, and begins to chase after the rest.

The Bonnet Carré spillway is another accident of the batture, an artifact of flood control decisions made nearly eighty years ago. In this case, the decision to put it here turned out to be a wise one and the U.S. Army Corps of Engineers, who built it, enjoys its moment once every few years when the gates are opened and a low sill of brown water a half-mile wide comes pouring safely through. What the Corps is more reluctant to tell you is that it resisted the notion of building a spillway here, or anywhere else on the Mississippi, for much of the previous half century, insisting on building ever bigger levees instead. It was a policy that, like a bad war, only led to greater investments and greater casualties when the big floods finally came. Not until 1927 when a massive surge took out the Corps' latest in levees and nearly erased New Orleans did the idea of escape valves like Bonnet Carré finally take root. The one I'm in now is about twenty miles upriver from the city as the crow flies. A larger spillway, and the ultimate safety net for the city and all of south Louisiana, is about fifty miles west of here on the Atchafalaya River. By a twist of fate, the Atchafalaya is the reason I live here now.

Spillways are like battures, dry in summer, wet in flood, and one of their side benefits is that they are undeveloped. It seems common sense to keep investments out of the place you are going to pass flood water, although that did not stop the mayor of New

Orleans, in a pre-Katrina moment, from proposing an international jetport in the Bonnet Carré spillway because the airport nearer the city was too small. Then again, the mayor's predecessor proposed building a similar airport in Lake Pontchartrain. Not next to the lake, *in* it. You don't understand, he told a colleague and me one Saturday morning when skepticism about his proposal started hitting the fan. This wasn't about an airport, he said, it was about getting three billion dollars to build it from the federal government. The mayor had a point, but so did we. It was a stupid place to put an airport.

The pressure to develop spillways, however, can be intense. All that land doing nothing. Years earlier, Louisiana caught the wave of Florida-style development, the kind that peddled lots in the Everglades to unsuspecting retirees from New York and Canada. A host of land companies sprang up around Lake Pontchartrain, the most aggressive of which was selling a particularly swampy stretch called Jones Island. Drive your boat right to your house, said the ads, smiling couples on dry land. The Sierra Club sent a pair of its members with a tape recorder, posing as buyers, to the site for a look-see. It was the Spring of 1973, with very high water on the Mississippi. Asked about what would happen to Jones Island if the Bonnet Carré Spillway were opened, the sales agent said not to worry, the Corps never used Bonnet Carré. They would stay high and dry. The next day the Corps opened the Bonnet Carré. The tape recording made its way to a federal agency recently established to police the Everglades shenanigans. The Jones Island venture collapsed.

What you have in the Bonnet Carré spillway then, instead of houses, is a lot of dogs. Not the small pets you see on the levee at the foot of Broadway, the city's free-range dating ground for canines and their owners. Out on the Bonnet Carré the dogs are black labs and setters, and they are being worked by hunters who throw out a red buoy, hold them close, and then blow the whistle for retrieve. The field on the upriver side of the spillway is full of whistles, shouts, and running dogs. In the center, though, is the model air show, and on a good afternoon a half-dozen men or more are at the controls, piloting homemade aircraft into takeoffs, rolls, and the maneuvers of aerial combat, the motors whining like angry wasps. These are impressive machines, gaily painted in reds, silver, and yellows with designs faithfully taken from *The Great Book of Aircraft*, all that work in the garage under florescent lightbulbs now rewarded in the freedom of a Saturday and an honest-to-God sky.

Today I am content to stay up on the river end of Bonnet Carré and watch the action as if it were a diorama, something done by two-inch people with quarter-inch dogs and bright insect machines. Off to my left, the Mississippi rolls unconcernedly by, and to my right, out of sight by four or five miles, are the waters of Lake Pontchartrain. The last time I was up here the spillway was open for the first time in many years and the Corps had provided industrial port-a-potties for people coming to watch. There was not much to see, just wide shallow water rushing by, but on the apron of the levee, by the spillway gates, the fishing was apparently superb. Lines of heron and egret, elegantly tall, were standing sentinel in the shallows, motionless, heads slightly forward, tracking something only they could see and then snatching down like a jackhammer and back up with a wiggling fish in their beaks, sideways. Which presented a problem, because no wading bird can swallow a fish sideways, and so this one reared back its elegant neck and tossed its catch into the air, daintily seizing it again by the head or tail and, arranged lengthwise now, swallowed it whole, a lump in the throat, a shudder of the breast, and done. Imagine learning that trick.

The heron were joined on the apron by a man in a sleeveless T-shirt with a number of tattoos and a fishing pole the size of a mast. When he cast, deep, all I saw was the large sinker and a bare hook and I thought, he's thrown off his bait. He did not sit and wait. Instead, he leaned his whole body forward and then back, sweeping his rod above him to jerk the line in several feet at a time, a quick reel to take up the slack, lean and jerk again. He came up empty, raised the rod to clear the weight and hook, and flung them out deep. I began to suspect that, moving so manically, fishing without bait, the man was a little unbalanced. This time, though, there was turmoil in the water, a big thrashing and flashes of smooth fish skin. Whatever he caught was too big to reel to shore. The man walked backwards up the apron pulling his rig, then walked back down reeling quickly, repeated the maneuver twice, gave one last tug, and there at the water's edge was a creature I'd never seen. What you catch in the Mississippi is flathead catfish, all the time. But this one had a head like an artillery shell. Buffalo fish, the man said as he unhooked it and kicked it back into the water. For about two seconds it lay there in shock, gave a single twist, and was gone. The man made another cast.

The Atchafalaya Spillway to the west of here has more buffalo fish, alligator gar, gaspargou, and other species you've never heard of than anywhere in the American South. The meanest by far is the gar, which can bite through your shoe. Alcide Verret, who lived out there, called it the choupique and said it mated with the opossum. It sneezed in her pouch with its long alligator snout, he explained, which is where she grew her babies.

The Atchafalaya Spillway will siphon half of the Mississippi River away from New Orleans at record flood, which is to say it matters. In the 1960s the Corps of Engineers was under heavy pressure to dredge the Atchafalaya and dry up the spillway for, of course, real estate development. It may sound a little crazy for a developer to put houses inside a floodway, but then they become someone else's problem. The newest subdivision was called Atchafalaya Acres. Right where half of the Mississippi River was to go at record flood.

It took time to change the army mind. In fact it took eighteen years. I fell into the fight. When the smoke cleared, I had moved down here to live, which is why I happened to be upriver this weekend morning with my head on the seat of my bicycle answering questions from a six-year-old about Jesus Christ. I still think about that little boy, and I still have no answers for him. The only thing about which I feel morally certain is that there is only one natural world and to screw it up is wrong. Although where that certainty comes from I cannot answer either.

EXPRESSWAY

We sit in a quiet courtyard overhung with plants and a flowering tree, utterly foreign. Although the day is hot they are both dressed in dark suits and narrow ties. They could be stockbrokers. We are at a wrought-iron table covered with glass. A fountain plays gently to the side. As we talk, a cockroach the size of a cigar crawls out from the garden, examines us, and crawls back in. They are unperturbed. To tell the truth they seem a little dazed, as if they still can't believe what they did. A couple of years earlier they and, at the beginning, a very few others had stopped an expressway along the Mississippi River batture against unthinkable odds.

I tell them about the Atchafalaya floodway to the west of the city, another mega-project by a construction agency that sits on the right hand of God. I want their advice. They listen, and pause before answering in the courteous manner of the South, a manner that at the time has me, coming from the North, wondering whether southerners have difficulty hearing questions. I know now, of course, that it is quite otherwise. Many southerners actually listen. After a five-count beat one of them, I think it was Borah, said, "Take your fight to Washington. You can never win here." It is what they did.

The Vieux Carré Expressway was going to transport the city of New Orleans into the twentieth century. A spur of Interstate 10, it would cut down to the river on Elysian Fields, wall off the Faubourg Marigny, and then rise over Jackson Square like an erector set, six lanes of cars and eighteen-wheelers on an elevated slab forty feet in the air. It was the darling of the mayor, city council, chamber of commerce, *Times-Picayune*, architectural firms, engineering firms, the state of Louisiana, and the federal Bureau of Public Roads, the largest building machine in the world. Nobody who was anybody opposed it. Pittsburgh, Chicago, San Francisco, New York, cities all across the country were lining the banks of their rivers with freeways. It was high time for New Orleans to catch up. The most historic city in America, tied to the Mississippi at birth and in every way since, was about to commit hari-kari.

Borah and Baumbach were not looking for trouble. Recent law graduates, they were having lunch at the Napoleon House one day where they casually asked the owner how things were going, and he said pretty bad, because of the new expressway. Borah remembers replying, "What's an expressway?" They knew nothing about highways, little more about public law, and had no clue about suing the federal government. Tulane didn't teach those things. But there are times in life when you suddenly know what you should be doing. This was theirs.

It was like Gandhi's march. It started with a small band of Quarter residents, ignored by city officials and press, and ended a few years later with public hearings that ran for seven hours at a stretch and packed in nearly a thousand people. Like many individuals who emerge from this kind of combat alive, but marked, Borah and Baumbach wrote their own history of the controversy, *The Second Battle of New Orleans*, a kind of exorcism of the wounds and ghosts. Theirs is the definitive book, except for two things which have more recently come to light. Each was in its own way an act of God, and without each of them the fate of the French Quarter, the tourism business in New Orleans, and many other things would be very different. For the worse.

The first God event was that the river spoke. For the previous one hundred years since Livingston's famous coup, New Orleans had been gradually sealing itself off from the Mississippi with, at first, a range of docks, then warehouses, then railroad tracks, and finally a twelve-and-a-half-foot flood control levee. There was not even a path across the batture, and if you somehow managed to wriggle your way down to the river, it was across railroad trestles and rotting piers to meet the washed-up trash and oil slick from a waterway that had forgotten the city as thoroughly as the city had forgotten the water. Back behind you in a separate world were the Faubourg Marigny and the Vieux Carré. Here on the bank you were now in transportation and pollution world. People forgot about the Mississippi. They couldn't even see it.

In 1962, as the expressway controversy was rising, geologists noted with alarm that the river was undercutting warehouses along batture that blocked it from the city. The most dangerous spot was by the Faubourg Marigny and the Vieux Carré. There was no option but to tear these structures down. Which was like lifting a veil. Suddenly, the demolition done, for the first time since the Civil War the people of New Orleans could view the Mississippi from Jackson Square. They could smell fresh water and feel the breeze. It quickened a distant pulse. From this moment forward the expressway controversy was not just about the impacts of interstate traffic on the Quarter, although they were going to be serious. It was also about something deeper that caught the imagination of everyone involved on up to members of the congressional delegation who had previously supported the expressway, and eventually, of all people, the federal secretary of transportation.

Local officials struggled in vain to come up with an acceptable plan for the riverfront location. Putting the expressway down in a trench presented obvious problems with flood control. Raising it in the air had its own difficulties. At the same time the Vieux Carré fight was going on, the state was building another elevated over Claiborne Avenue that would blight the city's most historic black community. The highway bureau offered to decorate the elevated across Jackson Square with quaint-looking street lamps. Unsurprisingly, it changed no minds. The final option was for six lanes of traffic at street level, but with several drawbacks, none the least of which was access to the rediscovered river. In his last few days in office, President Johnson approved federal funding for the Vieux

Carré Expressway. A few months later, the Nixon administration canceled it. Nixon's transportation secretary, John Volpe, had been the owner of the largest construction firm in the state of Massachusetts, and president of the General Association of Contractors. How could he do such a thing?

There is rarely a sole reason for anything in this world, but among those working here was the fact that the expressway planners had managed, by proposing an additional spur down historic Napoleon Avenue, to activate what one historian has called "the magnolia curtain," the silk-stocking residents of the Garden District, many of whom were Republicans, Nixon supporters, all of whom were firm about the city's historic past. Another factor was new legislation that answered to national anger over the federal highway program by imposing first-ever limits, including the protection of historic areas such as the Vieux Carré. A lawsuit generated by Borah and Baumbach hung over the expressway like an infected tooth, promising at the very least extended delay.

Then came another act of God, without which the fight could not have been won. Early on in the controversy, with few supporters, no finances, and uptown New Orleans still on the sidelines, Borah and Baumbach wrote a letter to Bishop Hannan of New Orleans. They requested an audience. They dared not say what about, for fear the door would close. But they thought that the expressway might be of concern to the bishop, as it ran about one hundred feet from the doors of St. Louis Cathedral.

Bishop Hannan met them in his office. The first thing they noticed was that he had a Washington, D.C., telephone book on his desk. He was connected to the outside world. They described the expressway over Jackson Square, fronting the cathedral. Hannan asked two questions. The first was, was this some kind of hoax? They assured him that it was not, it was real and going forward. The second was, and it was a jaw-dropper: "What do we need to do?" Neither of them had an answer prepared, Hannan's response was simply too fortuitous, but thinking rapidly they said they needed planning experts, traffic engineers, a consultant to develop an alternative plan. Who might that be? The bishop was friendly but disconcertingly direct. They said that Arthur D. Little of Boston had a fine reputation. The bishop cracked a thin smile and picked up the telephone. They waited, with no idea what was coming next.

He was calling Arthur D. Little. The CEO of the firm was U.S. Army General (retired) James D. Gavin, who had commanded the famed 82nd Airborne Division during the allied invasion of Europe. By a stunning coincidence, Hannan had served under Gavin as troop chaplain in four of these campaigns, including the Battle of the Bulge, in which the 82nd suffered terrible losses. Borah and Baumbach knew none of this at the time. Hannan asked to speak with General Gavin. They heard a voice on the other end of the line, and then Hannan said, "Hello, Jim? This is Phil!" They looked at each other in wonder. They were in.

By the end of the call, Arthur D. Little had a team ready to come to New Orleans the following Monday. By yet another coincidence, the city's leading philanthropist Edgar Stern had also called Borah and Baumbach, and this time he was the one requesting a meeting. Visiting his offices over a noon hour, Borah remembered passing a kitchen in which ladies were cooking steaks for lunch. This was a very New Orleans revolution. They left the meeting with the promise of funding. Stern had backed the civil rights movement throughout the South and, at a time when other southern cities were exploding in demonstrations and police riots, he, and Hannan separately, met with New Orleans leaders, persuading them to accept the fact of integration. In words that Bishop Hannan would often use later in support of other public causes, it was "the right thing to do." The rest is history.

We were incredibly lucky. As other American cities struggle to reconnect with their rivers again through mazes and walls of concrete, ours was here waiting for us like a patient lover from a fairy tale. All she needed was to be seen.

Many years following, several New Orleans mayors and city councils come and gone, I happened to be standing at a reception on the top of the Jax Brewery with Jerome Glazer, a Damon Runyonesque figure who had been part of the fabric of New Orleans for much of his adult life, with many good works and even an airport access road to his name. Jerry was chewing on an unlit cigar and scanning the scene below, the boats on the river, the cathedral in the square, and the hum of the city as it revved up for the evening. I mentioned that it was a lovely evening. In stead of agreeing, he gazed out at the scene with deep disappointment and said, "It's a damn shame!" And then, pointing down, he looked at me as if I were the one who spoiled it and added, "You know, we could have had that expressway right there! It would have been so beautiful."

I did not want to offend the man. But I could not think of a thing to say.

ELVIS

"The owls, they'll eat your *dog!*" Ricky says, poking the fire with a stick.

I say I didn't know that.

"Hell, yes," he explains, "come right down and take 'em away."

I say a man I know over by the Atchafalaya shoots owls because he says they take his chickens, but taking dogs is news to me.

"Oh, yeah," he says, as if it happens several times a week.

We are both listening for another call. One had sounded upriver, not too far, and that's what triggered the conversation. It was a barred owl, the one that looks like a sack of laundry in a tree, and they tend to start calling right at sunset as their night vision kicks in and they are getting ready to hunt. Sometimes they chatter back and forth to each other in hoo-hoos and haw-haws like an argument of crows. Come pure dark, though, like coyotes and other wild things that need to get serious about catching something to eat, they quiet down.

I say I wonder how they *eat* a dog, and he says, "Skin 'em, like a catfish," and I say that sounds pretty complicated. Poking the fire again, he says, "Owls are *smart*," adding as a clincher, "Ever see their beak?"

I was, however, sidetracked onto skinning catfish, and how many people knew that you skinned them at all. I mean, if you were starving and someone gave you a big catfish from the river, what would you do? The skin is the consistency of a Goodyear tire and it clings to the flesh like superglue. What they do is nail the catfish to a tree, head up, cut a ring around the neck, and then pull the skin down over the body with a pair of pliers like a pair of tight jeans. The nail had better be secure because it is more of a battle than shaving the family cat. I see nails in the trees along the river bank sometimes. My thought is that, given a catfish, I'd probably still starve.

The owl sounds off again, this time farther away. The call is unmistakable, a burst of hoots that rise like a question mark and then fall into sadness. It is the call you hear in the lost-in-the-woods movies where scared teenagers huddle in their tents until the monster creeps a hairy foot inside. But what I hear more is loneliness. As long as people believe that this bird kills their dogs, then barred owls have a problem.

On the other hand, at least they are around. The pelicans are back, too, bred from recruits from Florida. They tend to favor water with a little more salt in it, but from time to time a line of them led by a silver-headed adult will come gliding up the Mississippi, rising and falling like a game of follow-the-leader, and you simply have to stop and look. Sometimes a bald eagle gets this far downriver, and where you are most likely to spot one is in the open, over the power lines, above the gulls, bigger than the vultures and circling absolutely motionless, unperturbed, the lion king of the sky. The bird you will not see here anymore is the one we have eliminated from all of these river bottoms and perhaps the world. It was the signature bird of the southern forests, the ivory-billed woodpecker, also called Elvis because your chances of seeing it now are about the same. And yet, I did. Or maybe I did, I'll never know. It was just east of here along the Mississippi River's little sister, the Pearl.

I blame my dog. The Pearl runs down from northern Mississippi to form the border with Louisiana, where it braids out and floods a wide forested swamp. The lower Mississippi used to look like this, too, and the early towns like New Orleans hugged the banks of natural levees and hung on. Back behind them in the flooded woods was a woodpecker so spectacular in its size and coloring that locals named it the Lord God! bird, because that is what people would exclaim when they saw it. It is intensely wild by nature, and James Audubon tells of one chained to a desk in a hotel room where it proceeded to destroy the desk leg, the its own leg, and die. The ivory bill lived in tall cypress trees past their prime, infected by grubs, and that was where she fed, hammered out her nesting holes, and raised her young.

We wiped them out. We shot them, of course; they were big and pretty so it was *not* hard to kill them, but, in the end, we cut down their trees. All of them. The last ivory-bill families were up in Avoyelles Parish, and their woods were logged to liquidate some debts of the Singer Sewing Machine company. One of the last people alive to see the Lord God bird was George Lowery, a young ornithologist at the time, who joined an expedition to record it in the 1930s. They got some grainy photographs and an even more grainy phonograph disk. The call on the disk went "Yank yank!" followed by a distinctive drumming. It was not machine-gun rapid like the pileated woodpecker, which is common in these parts, but a slow, loud couplet, like two sledge hammers on a log. The bird was not seen again. But it is the call that matters here.

By the 1950s Lowery was a leading ornithologist at LSU. Visiting the state wildlife agency one day, he heard a conversation about the ivory bill, whose mystique had lingered on, and he remarked that they were extinct. "That's not so," said another visitor who happened by. "I've got 'em on my place by Alexandria." Lowery said that it wasn't possible, which would have ended things except that the following week the same man showed up at his office and dropped a dead ivory bill on his desk. He'd shot it that morning. Proof, the old, incontrovertible way, that they were still on this earth. No others were ever found.

More than a decade later, Lowery received another visit, this time from a man who had two photographs of an ivory bill on a tree. Lowery was unable to confirm the sightings, but he presented the photos as evidence of the bird's possible existence at the next meeting of the American Ornithologist' Union, the supreme court for all matters pertaining. This is a conservative body, as it should be, skepticism is how science proves its theories, and it treated

Lowery's photographs roughly. Some said that they showed dummies on a tree. The question of the photographs was never resolved. Lowery died not long afterwards, and the ivory-bill woodpecker retreated again to the obit section of the news.

It simply would not stay there. In the 1990s a hunter reported seeing one by the Pearl River. It was not an ordinary siting. The hunter was a graduate student at LSU, an NRA member, and the kind of fellow who went hunting in order to be in the woods. He described characteristics of the bird he saw that were not open source material, but were in the notes of those who had last seen it up on the Singer tract a half century before. As a matter of genetics alone, the survival of the ivory bill seemed impossible; a population that limited could not escape the death spiral of inbreeding and mutations over so many generations. But here was the report. Nikon funded a search throughout the lower Pearl. National Public Radio visited the search team, and that broadcast came to me one morning when I was standing in the bathroom shaving.

I remember the moment as clearly as if it happened today, twelve years later. When I turned on the radio, I'd heard none of the run up to the story. They were playing a recording taken in the Pearl just a few weeks earlier. It did not have the yank yank! call, which would have been dispositive, but it had caught, several times, the slow, loud couplet of a hammer on trees. I had heard the Singer tract recording which included this couplet; it was on a record I'd listened to once when I was very ill, and it was grooved into my brain like the multiplication tables. When that same sound came over the radio, I dropped my razor into the washbasin and said, holy shit! so loudly that Lisa called out to see if I was hurt. I was not hurt. I was in wonderland.

So we went into the Pearl River swamp to look for it, my friend Jay in his canoe, and my dog and I in ours. Ms. Bear is not too good at seeing birds; for one, they are usually up too high in the trees, but she can sense an animal before I do and that, too, is important to what happened. It was late spring but the Pearl runs more on local rainfall than the Mississippi does, and it had rained a lot. You could paddle just about anywhere on the high brown water, moving swiftly, more like a river through trees. We crossed the forest entirely from west to east, often out of sight of each other, lost in the scene, thick yellow-top at water level topped by red maple seeds, green cypress trees in the background, under a blue sky. The primary colors of our lives.

By mid-afternoon we had drifted into a lake that we could not locate on our maps. Jay saw a fisherman in the distance and drifted over to him to get our bearings. That is when I heard it, two distinct chops, loud as two sledgehammers and very close by. Not daring to breathe, I kept my paddle in the water and feathered the canoe slowly to point towards the sound. There was a total silence, and then an answering rap, two strikes, at a considerable distance, deep in the trees. I pushed the canoe towards a tiny cove in the trees, Ms. Bear alert on the bow like a black hood ornament, she had heard something, too, maybe scented it, who knows what she knew. Then it happened again, very close ahead, a loud double blow, no machine gun, a pause, and then two answers way out in the distance. At this point I was in the cove, and the sound seemed to be coming from low near the water, straight ahead, around the spread of a wide buttonbush. The water was quiet here and littered with floating branches. I began poking the nose of the canoe past the bush; Ms. Bear could already see beyond, I had about four feet to go, and just then a turtle to the side slid off its log with a loud plop! It startled Bear, who gave a small woof! which in turn startled whatever was ahead of us because it rose with a huge rush of wings straight up through the trees and I saw no color, only a shape, fast, and it was gone.

I sat still and listened for several minutes. Jay came back. I asked whether he had seen anything, and he said no but he had heard the two raps. We examined the far side of the buttonbush and found a crooked stump up out of the water, torn up by something. A large bill.

The next day I called up an ivory-bill expert at LSU and asked him about the double raps. He said it was probably an accident.

There were Navy SEALs practicing out there, he told me, and it could be that they had heard about the Nikon recordings and were playing tricks on people, pounding on trees. I think I said something like "anything's possible," not knowing whether I meant the SEALs or the bird. To be sure, some things are not possible. It is just hard to say which things they are.

I will tell you this, though. The pull of this one bird is so strong that there are thousands of us, maybe millions, who would go down on our knees and promise never to do this to such a creature again if we knew the ivory-bill woodpecker were still alive. Just give us another chance. We would not even have to see it. Seeing it is not the point.

STATUE

You rarely see women on the batture, at least down in the woods. I can only remember two, over the years. One was camped in a small sea of wine cartons near the water intake for Ochsner Hospital, where the helicopters fly in low with emergency cases from the rigs offshore, casualties from another kind of war. It is an expedited drill; the ambulance is waiting on the landing pad before the vehicle sets down, and the stretcher is offloaded and en route to the hospital doors before the big blades have stopped rotating. The wine lady had a tarp stretched under a sycamore tree. She looked at me like I was coming to evict her, so my dog and I just moved on by, not even hello. The second woman I saw more recently. She was much younger and she was making love.

I had no idea what she was doing at the time. I didn't even know that she was a human being. I thought she was part of a statue, along with the other sculpture you find south of the power lines in the late spring. This is where a Tulane professor brings his sculpture class for an exam in found art, and, while some of their projects barely stand up for the afternoon, others last through the summer and into the fall, losing out over time to the wind and the occasional forage for firewood.

With luck you could be cruising by on the levee on exam day and down towards the river young men and women are erecting a pole like the flag on Iwo Jima. Only this is the third pole and they could signify anything from the solar clocks at Stonehenge to the crosses at Galilee; their impact lies in the answer we give to them going by. Closer yet to the water is a hut made of sticks that beaver have gnawed from the willow trees, tied together with fishing line. Then come several contraptions of driftwood enhanced by nylon tow rope, plastic Coke carriers, and Playmate coolers, all broken in some way but made of materials that will outlast the time of man on this planet by a million years. Last spring I happened to see the professor arrive for inspection, at which point an enterprising team lit its structure on fire, throwing what I hope was not gasoline on top of it, and the effect was spectacular. Here is something you are not likely to see upstream across the parish line.

There is more to find weeks later as the waters recede, some of great value although you would be hard pressed to go out and sell it. Whole trees come downriver stripped of their bark and sand-rubbed by the silt, and they wash up, large and small, near the hospital where the Mississippi makes an abrupt turn. A friend of mine who lives on the batture found a cypress log floating in his backyard and lassoed it with a cable to keep it from washing away. As the water dropped he beached it, and for the next year he hollowed it out with nothing more than a sharpened adze to make a dugout canoe, smooth as a baby's bottom with high curls fore and aft. He has yet to launch it and perhaps he never will. The trip was in the journey. But if he does launch, I want him to be wearing a life jacket with a line to land, which I'll have cinched around a tree.

I have been known to bring pieces of the smaller driftwood home, to the point that Lisa has declared a no-net-new-stuff policy; for every find I have to throw out an old one. On the front porch, though, we have hung a perfect cross of wood twisted like muscles, as if it, too, suffered crucifixion. And on a washed-up cable spool about three feet high we have inverted the lower trunk of a small tree with its roots like the bodies of serpents, sun-bleached silver when I discovered it, quite by accident, because I couldn't get my dog away from whatever she was into at the water line.

Going into the woods the show continues, and this is what confused me so much when I stumbled on the young woman. Here at the edge of the trees are more products of the art class, mobiles of bottles and strips of metal hung from the branches and arranged to bump each other as they turn. Close your eyes and you could be on the patio of Ted Turner's mansion on the cliffs of Malibu, wind chimes in the breeze. Instead you are stepping over the poison ivy and there is no clear ground to lie on in these woods below the hospital, which is why if you are going to have sexual intercourse here you are pretty much going to be standing up.

It happened when Ms. Bear and I were coming upriver, and following the path so succinctly that we were making no noise at all. About to round a mulberry bush that screened the view ahead, but not completely, I saw a wrought-iron statue that surprised me because iron is not a common find around here. It was a jet black and sinewy structure, and there was no doubt that it was a work of art, because it stood out from the trees by itself, shaped like a triangle, one long column and a shorter one which seemed bent double and clasping its ankles like a diver in the pike position. I thought immediately of the sculpture students, and that they had really outdone themselves this time. It even seemed to beat with the slightest pulse of breath, but it was otherwise as frozen as a museum work, elegant.

The dog broke the ice. She had stopped, too, perceiving long before I that we had a couple of humans here, and she needed to get their drift before going forward. Now she was ready, and giving a small "woof" she padded around the tree and towards what she probably hoped was food or at least a pat on the head. By this time I'd also figured out that these were two human beings, completely naked, he entering her from behind like the Greek statues they do not show you at the Acropolis, or the work of Robert Mapplethorpe. I would have backed away and left them but the dog was already out there, and so I stepped out, too.

Without saying a word the couple, who could not have been past their early teens, pulled apart. She drew a sheath dress that she had tucked behind her neck down over her body in one move while he slipped his pants up as if they were stockings, no fumbling by either one. I tried not to look at them, moving by, telling my dog to move, and it was only later that I realized that I was wearing binoculars around my neck for spotting birds. What these youngsters must have thought seeing a white man emerge from the bushes with binoculars I can only imagine.

I told Lisa about it that evening and how, after I got over my surprise, how right I thought it was. I mean, I said, human beings have been copulating out-of-doors a lot longer than they have indoors, and even the indoor ones have only found anything like privacy in the last blink of an eye of history. Besides, I added, warming to the task, you and I at a younger age found sex in the back seats of cars or over at a friend's house, but suppose you were fifteen and didn't have a car or know anyone with a spare room? Wouldn't you go down to the woods?

Lisa was unimpressed. "He is going to get her pregnant," she said, and she should know because she is a social worker and deals with the before and after of teenagers on a regular basis. "He is not just fornicating with her," she continued, "he is fornicating with her life." Would it make any difference if he were using a condom, I asked. "I doubt he was using a condom," she said, and she was doubtless correct here, too.

But I cannot help it. I still remember what I saw in the woods that day as if I'd been looking at two brilliant dragonflies, the kind you see around the water; he is on top of her, their wings are shimmering, this is their moment, and they are flying off to who knows where.

LOW WATER

IT IS LATE FALL NOW, the sun has just set, and the river shines through the bare trees. The power plant on the west bank is outlined by the lights on its tanks and platforms, and behind them dark grain elevators reach their chutes down to an empty dock. Upstream are the shadows of the Huey Long Bridge and the Avondale shipyard. The air smells lightly industrial. There is nobody in sight. Judging from the horizon, we could be in northern New Jersey.

Suddenly, around the bend comes a mirage, a wedding cake structure on the water, three full decks, candles blazing, smoke belching from black stacks, and the faint sound of a band. Sticking out from its rear end like a bustle is a large paddle wheel, churning water. Then, around its rear comes another wedding cake, also ablaze, but with its paddle wheels on the sides, churning equally vigorously. Over the sound of its band come the laughs and cheers of the passengers crowding the rail who, having left the port of New Orleans at least an hour ago, are well into their third drinks. It is the race of the *American* and the *Delta Queen*.

I stop dead. Dimming my eyes makes the power plant and the grain elevators disappear. The levee blacktop fades. I am on a steamboat pounding up the river, watching the land go by. I see the sky over the river blacken with the flight of a thousand birds, ducks beyond counting, the wind of their wings reaching me, the unimaginable past so close in time and so far away.

Driving up along the river road you see buildings. Traveling the levee top, you see ghosts. The legacy of Edward Livingston falls behind, then a chain of wharves and warehouses that have privatized the river up to an abrupt terminus, Audubon Park. This urban green, the site of a plantation too swampy to survive, embroiled in a land scandal so thick it wound up impeaching the Governor in Baton Rouge, was then ceded to the World Cotton Exposition of 1884, which promptly went out of business. The land defaulted to the city, which turned to the nephew of America's greatest landscape architect, Frederick Olmstead, for a plan. Young Olmstead shared his uncle's passion for natural spaces and eschewed their conversion to sporting arenas. He designed a commons with ponds, gardens, and wooded walkways. The city wasted little time converting the plan to baseball fields and other amusements, dominated by a golf course.

Olmstead's other dream, however, was to extend the park to the Mississippi River for public enjoyment. At the time, the batture between the park and the river was a city dump filled with coal ash and discarded appliances, which turned out to be a good thing. It required less mud from the river to top the fill, and the Audubon Butterfly, our first window on the river in a century, was born.

On the upstream edge of what is now the park lay Camp Louis, built by the Confederate army in 1861 with its troop tents raised on platforms and fresh water pumped in from boats on the river for five hundred dollars a week. On July 4 of its inaugural year, with war still just an exciting prospect on the horizon, Camp Louis held a "grand review" with dress parades and mock maneuvers that attracted more than ten thousand visitors. Military spectacle was in vogue. One year later, so many socialites from Washington, D.C., flocked out in their carriages to the Virginia countryside to watch the first battle of Manassas that, after the unexpected debacle, they choked the roads leading home, leaving the Union troops vulnerable to their Confederate pursuers. War was a different idea in 1861 but, when one thinks of the slaughter at Antietam and Cold Harbor to come, not for long.

Leaving the park, you are in Greenville and the Union barracks that recruited the first black regiment of the Civil War. With the opening of a new war on American Indians to the west, the Greenville barracks became home to the famed Buffalo Soldiers under General Philip Sheridan. Black cavalry trained at Greenville went after Geronimo, Sitting Bull, Pancho Villa, and other enemies of color, and then on to prosecute a war of extermination in the Philippines. As Frederick Douglass saw it, once the black man got his "brass letters," he could no longer be denied. How Douglass would, today, see that same participation in what was, at the least, raw conquest and in some cases pure genocide is a question in the air, going by.

You can also, if you close your eyes and concentrate, hear Mahalia Jackson singing, first along the docks at Walnut Street, then in the churches of Greenville and the Black Pearl. And one final glorious time in September 1963 on the mall in Washington, D.C., where she opened with a spiritual before half a million people, civil rights marchers, and when finally the last in a string of speakers, a preacher, stood to add his bit she turned to him and said, "Tell them about the dream, Martin." And the preacher did. This is where she came from, a cheek-by-jowl, black-and-white New Orleans neighborhood that seems impossible to people who do not live here.

Living together was one thing, of course, and mixing was another. Mahalia Jackson worked summers at the swimming pool in Audubon Park but she was not allowed in the water. When the pool was later integrated by court order the park, rather than comply, let it decay beyond repair. Then closed it entirely. This, too, lingers in the air.

The Jackson house sat on the levee side of the railroad tracks. She later recalled that you could be inside and see the sky through the roof, and when it rained they ran around with buckets to catch it. Like her neighbors, she scratched the riverbank for firewood which she dried out and sold for pennies, saving some to keep the house warm in winter. The next community upstream was called Pension Town because of the number of veterans and retirees. Hers was called Pinching Town, as in they squeezed every bit out of a dollar, and each vendor of merchandise had a different song. Going by on the levee, one is passing through a force field that took a black woman from this place and put her before American presidents and the heads of state of Europe. It wasn't just her voice. Whatever it also was, that is what you feel. Every time I get depressed about the way the world is, I come across a person.

Across the levee from the Jackson home, long gone now, not even a plaque, begins the batture domain of the Bisso family which, starting with a modest ferry across the Mississippi to Gretna, launched an empire of tugboats, salvage operations, and the largest coal port in the region. There was plenty to salvage. The Army Corps has since discovered the wrecks of nineteen vessels along the Bisso stretch of the river alone, less than a mile long. In the spring of 1891 Bisso's ferry business got an extra boost when high water blew out the levee on the west bank, sending a torrent through the Ames Crevasse. The water stayed up for months, and the crevasse soon became a tourist attraction. The Bissos had to add boats to carry people out to witness the great flow. There were no news reels or television in those days. You went to see things for yourself.

We have gone less than five hundred yards. Now we have to drop towards the railroad tracks to skirt the Corps of Engineers building that stands like a monstrous packing crate on its own domain. Inside are three floors of the largest assemblage of office cubicles in Louisiana, tasked with what has turned out to be Mission Quagmire, the management of the lower Mississippi River. Whether the Corps can rework its former canal and levee projects in a way that restores a sinking Louisiana, and whether we will allow them to, given all the competing dependencies that cling to these projects like vines, is the biggest question Hurricane Katrina left behind. We do not even have the answers on paper yet.

I first visited these Corps buildings in August of 1971, on a day so oppressive that when my plane landed in Baton Rouge there was not a single thing moving outside. Not a car. Not a bird in the sky. I drove down Airline Highway to the city through walls of rosocane ten feet high backed by the flares from the riverside refineries, wondering what manner of people would choose to live here. I was bringing a deal struck with the Corps headquarters in Washington about restudying the Atchafalaya Floodway, the largest project in the District's basket at the time. I was about as welcome as Dr. Death. Nobody messed with the Atchafalaya project, and nobody messed with the New Orleans Corps. What I thought was to be a personal meeting with the district colonel turned out to be an audience of some fifty Corps employees, for whom I may have been a first sighting of something called an environmentalist. This I remember about the meeting. The colonel sat next to me, and as I was speaking drew a two-inch rectangle on his paper pad. He spent the rest of my presentation filling in the rectangle until it shone, over and over, never once straying from the box.

Picking up the pace now, we pass by the Black Pearl neighborhood, celebrated in the city's signature novel, A Confederacy of Dunces, now fighting a set of high-rise condominiums which would block it from the river, and then on to Carrollton, still a town of its own and the end of what is left of the trolley line. Where Carrollton meets the levee stood a railroad station in gothic stone, the Original Southport Club, and then on into Jefferson Parish and the railroad ferry with boats so large they carried four boxcars at a time across the Mississippi to the west bank and the interior of America beyond.

Moving more rapidly out River Road, we find Teoulete's grocery and pharmacy on its corner facing the levee. Across the road was the neighborhood of Shrewsbury, black facing white, and not many people crossed that road. Teoulet's, also called Towe's—both names are still on the front—had fifteen-cent movies in the rear on weekends and its own share of violence as well. There are stories of killings. There is a rumor of a hanging.

The Marsalis motel in Shrewsbury was one of the few accommodations for black musicians during the Great Depression, the heartbeat of New Orleans jazz. One of their songs was called "Shrewsbury Blues." Martin Luther King stayed there. So did civil rights attorney Thurgood Marshall and one of America's first black congressmen since reconstruction, Adam Clayton Powell, more ghosts feeding into the most diverse musical family in the history of New Orleans, which is saying a mouthful. But how many families count five world-class musicians, none of them playing the same instrument? You are passing their roots.

The Marsalis motel is now gone, an empty lot. Teoulet's grocery is now an after-work watering hole and a weekend hangout for Harley-Davidsons and Saints fans. Across the road what is left of black Shrewsbury lives its own life. Even today, few people cross.

Coming back downriver, I am still seeing the the race of the steamboat queens. They have disappeared around the bend, but in my mind's eye a hundred steamers line the docks at New Orleans, Walnut Street and Carrollton landings, moored so closely together they look like cows in the chutes. Others ply the river, passing keelboats, skiffs, and rafts. I can see the red heat of their boilers and the white plume of their steam. It is a terribly attractive picture, and I wish I could be there.

This evening I find myself reading a book by Hodding Carter about the lower river. He, too, is reminiscing about things he had read of but never seen, and he describes the diversions of the first-class passengers, safe on the upper deck of these same steamboats. They would drop pieces of food to the cargo handlers and crew on the lower level, watching them "scramble like animals" for the scraps. Before a drop they would shout, sportingly, "Grub pile!"

There are several lower Mississippi Rivers.

PARISH LINE

AT THE BOUNDARY between Orleans and Jefferson Parish the rail-road line leaves River Road and heads inland. The batture looks the same on both sides, but it is pretty much where east meets west and that line extends down to the water. I walk up here in winter when the underbrush has died back to stretch the dog and to look for hawks, which are easy to spot in the bare trees, but I am always aware that I've crossed the parish line. Jefferson is the only place I have been given a ticket for the offense of dog-off-the-leash.

Ms. Bear and I were well into the woods, but here came the levee policeman climbing out of his vehicle and down the embankment with his citation book in hand, asking for my driver's license. I said, "For my dog?" and that's when he knew and I knew that I was going to get a ticket. They run a tight ship up there. I'll say this, I feel safe, but it is a trade-off. Another time they stopped me on the levee path for bicycling no-handed. I have bad shoulders and so I can't stay down on the handle bars for long. I thought about arguing this case, too, because I doubt that there is a no-hands law on the books. In south Louisiana, though, you can go to jail for arguing with a policeman, even if you're white, which some of my students find out every year. The ones who are black already know it.

The batture in Jefferson is a good walk because the woods are deeper here, and there is no one around. In the spring an occasional family will walk along the fringe of the trees with a plastic pail looking for berries, but farther in there is not even a path. To curb whatever impulse to wander may linger in the modern mind, the Jefferson levee board has posted large red stop signs reading No Trespassing every few hundred yards. A spokesman explained that it was a public safety measure due to "ponds, sinkholes, and limbs dangling from trees" in there. One thinks immediately of an unwitting traveler, struck by a tree limb, falling into quicksand and slowly disappearing so that all that remains is his hat and the protruding fingers of one hand.

I actually took a moment to write the levee spokesman a polite note saying that I'd been walking through those woods for twenty years and I'd seen one small snake but no dangerous sinkholes. I had seen holes dug up by wild pigs looking for roots to eat. From the number of holes there must be a whole family of pigs up there, but they are shy as phantoms. I caught a glimpse of them in the fog one morning; they resembled miniature mastodons trotting away. The only time I ever worried about my dog was when she took off after some pigs that she must have scented and I found her later, disconsolate, looking out over a swamp where their tracks went in and disappeared.

There was a time when Jefferson Parish was more laissez-faire about life. Within the memory of senior citizens it outdid New Orleans as the sin city of the South. Those halcyon days finally yielded to a spasm of good government that drove the gaming underground, at which critical juncture the civil rights movement swept into New Orleans like a hurricane, sending waves of families across the parish line. These were hard-working, law-abiding, and Sunday-praying citizens who would help you at the drop of a hat. They just could not face the prospect of sharing life with black people. With integration, even the legendary Pontchartrain Beach with its Zephyr rollercoaster and dance halls featuring Louis Prima and the Tommy Dorsey Band, only a ten-cent trolley ride from town, closed down.

For the next four decades the most popular elected official across the parish line was Sheriff Harry Lee, who made his feelings about New Orleans plain. At one point he started barricading roads that lead into Jefferson to keep out undesirables, and on another he announced that if he saw black men riding in "rinky-dink automobiles" around neighborhoods where they didn't belong he would arrest them. One letter to the editor suggested that he issue visas. Race relations along the parish line may be little different from the way they are in most of America, just more patent, but the fact is that you see no blacks along the Mississippi batture here for several miles.

But there are lots of kids. They will be on small, fat-tired bicycles pedaling furiously down the slope of the levee and into the trees on paths that they have modified with ramps, high jumps, water holes, and all the risks that make life a thrill. One route takes the bikers straight at a No Trespassing sign and then veers off at the very last minute, as if it were trying to frighten the sign itself with the threat of collision. It would certainly frighten the spokesman at the levee board. Farther into the woods there are rope swings and tree platforms, projects that petrified me as a boy because making things was fun but being more than three feet off the ground turned me to stone. Walking by today I can feel the dare of childhood in these woods as strongly as I feel the utter freedom of no parents and no rules but the ones we made, and although our rules could be brutal it was still a good trade. Besides, where else would we have been? Facebook and Grand Theft Auto hadn't been invented yet. In that sense I imagine we were deprived.

Prowling the batture in Jefferson, I am looking for the remains of a fire. How can you be in the woods and not build a fire? Granted, my brother and I and Mason Ahearn started one in a field up the street one day that blew out of control and nearly reached the Esso gas station. The only way I dodged that bullet was by running home to squeal on them to my parents. Still, I try to imagine a world in which the adults in charge have never made a fire from scratch or been out in the woods at all except when accompanied by a qualified guide. It seems bleak. I try to believe that this new breed of woods-less people will take care of the natural world anyway, but I don't see why they would. If you don't feel something then it does not come up on your radar. I see people like this every day who probably think I am from another planet, and they are right. My planet is called earth.

The other thing I look for is traps, because there are a lot of small creatures out here and their sign is everywhere. When I was young my schoolmate Peter came across an old edition of *The American Boy's Handy Book* and we committed its marvels to memory. Written in the 1880s, its instructions were so dated they could not be followed faithfully. A section on crossbows began: take an ordinary barrel stave. We had never seen a barrel stave. But the chapter that enchanted us was on deadfalls and snares, which we tried out with materials from the garage and then moved into the woods along Route 22 in northern New Jersey, our batture at the time, now the site of a Chinese take-out and an emporium called Tire Man, whose long, robotic arms composed of rubber tires stretch out over the windshields of passing cars to beckon them in. But before the advent of such refinements these woods were the great escape, and that is where we ran our trap line.

I was the cheering section. Peter had the patience to work over the trigger mechanisms to the point that they held the tension of a bent tree but were still delicate enough to spring when a squirrel took the bait, which in our case was peanut butter. We went out every day after school for most of two winters to find our traps sprung, deadfalls down, bait taken, but no animal. Then one week we caught two of them, a dead squirrel and a live beagle. Skinning the squirrel took some of the zest out of it for me, but finding the beagle broke the magic altogether. The dog was caught by its neck in a snare and had spent hours hopping on its hind legs, leaving a little circle of pain on the snow. We released it and walked home through a new subdivision that was beginning to climb the hill from the east, knowing that this part of our lives was ending. Not just for us.

What saddens me in these woods along the Mississippi is that there are not more signs of boy. I say boy and cringe because I know how sexist that sounds, but the cold fact is that I never saw girls in the woods when I was growing up, and I rarely do now. The dynamics for non-boy are as different as they are for non-white. You are very alone out here, even if the woods are not extensive, and within the memory of our elders white men brought blacks down to the river and killed them. God knows what they did when they found a female.

One spring weekend I was canoeing with my students through the Atchafalaya swamp west of here. Norman was in my bow, brown-skinned in a tawny way that until you got up close might, in the terrible vernacular of the region, pass. We were drifting down a lake when suddenly an aluminum johnboat came roaring out of the trees, two white men in it, the one in front holding a shotgun about twice the length of anything I'd used in the army, draped across his knees. They stopped in front of us, their wake sending our canoes rocking crazily, we a little out of control, they very much in control, and they said you are trespassing on our property.

Now here is another set of people you do not argue with in Louisiana, two men with a gun, and so I said we were glad to see them because we had gotten lost, which seemed to mollify them. Then the fellow in the bow noticed Norman. He focused in like an owl on a mouse. "Well, well," he said, about ten feet from us and looking Norman straight in the eyes, "my granddaddy used to bring niggers out here and shoot 'em." Dead silence in the canoes. Dead silence in the johnboat, only the gurgle of its motor on idle. Then Norm spoke up, brightly, like the kid in the front row who had just guessed the right answer. "How times change!" and he flashed his best smile. No smiles in the johnboat, but there were far too many witnesses around for violence, so the two men wheeled it around and gunned the motor, sending us rocking again but free. All the rest of us were white, but we had felt for a brief moment what it was like to be on the other side of the line.

Jefferson Parish is not Atchafalaya country by a long shot, but it is something of a bridge to a past that remains constantly present. The entire state of Louisiana is. You can drive a long way away from New Orleans in any direction before it feels less humid.

SOUTHPORT

On November 27, 1940, the front page of the *New Orleans Item* carried two headline stories. One was an interview with the Duchess of Windsor, then residing in Nassau with the man who abdicated the throne of England to marry her. She talked discreetly about his drinking problem.

The other headline read, "Death Calls the Turn on Rudy O'Dwyer, One of Fabulous Figures." It was a charming story, basically about Rudy's menagerie of rare birds behind his house on Monticello Street, just off the batture, with homage to his public service and generosity. He endowed St. Agnes Church on Jefferson Highway. He provided the lobby for Madonna Manor. He gave fire engines to the fire department, college tuitions to neighborhood boys, clothes and food to the poor. The second page of the story is accompanied by a full-length photograph captioned, "Colorful Figure Dies." Among other things, Rudy also owned the "fastest cabin cruiser in local waters," and his aviary of three thousand species drew grammar school classes and movie divas the likes of Marlene Dietrich and Mae West. Nothing second class.

Rudy's funeral was attended by judges, fruit stand vendors, businessmen, legislators, and the political elite of the parish—all of which spoke of money. The article made passing reference to his ownership of the Original Southport Club on the batture at the parish line. It was one of the most successful gambling operations in Louisiana, which is no small accolade.

You can't miss the place from the levee path. The Original Southport was built at the very foot of the grass berm and was run by the Irish. The New Southport, which superseded it, just across the road, was run by the Marcello family of the Cosa Nostra. These days Southport Hall announces itself every weekend with a blast of sound from rockabilly bands whose music is actually easier to discern from the levee top than it is on the club's deck—the size of a basketball court—and a parking lot for two hundred pickup trucks at a time. The young men and women strutting the premises are drinking beer and playing bad on a spot that, not too long ago, really *was* bad, at least in the eyes of those in the federal government to whom gambling was a serious crime. But not in all eyes, by a long shot.

Louisiana is ambivalent about many rules that are taken for granted elsewhere in America, which is a good thing, but the one about which it has been absolutely schizophrenic is gambling. Over the years, the basic approach has been to ban it completely and to enjoy it immensely. The early arriving French Creoles were so addicted to the sport that they were said to have walked off the boats with a deck of cards and a roulette wheel in each hand. Every dive in the growing city offered some form of faro or keeno, bingo-like games that involved a crowd, to which the riverboat gamblers later added three-card monte and other small-group sleights of hand. The great New Orleans gambling halls in the 1800s rivaled theatres and ballrooms in décor, but by the end of the century the business came under the control of two organizations, the Sicilian Matranga family and an Irish boss of several clubs named Joe Hyland. What ensued was inevitable.

In the 1890s, the Matrangas got embroiled in a Sicilian turf war with the Provenzano family, leading to the bloodiest mob killing spree in American history. Before the end of the century the police would ascribe one hundred murders to the feud, prompting New Orleans police chief David Hennessy, an Irishman, to step in. It was a fatal decision. Hennessy was gunned down in the open street by Matranga henchmen. That was another fatal decision. An angry mob of citizens stormed the parish prison, killed several Matrangas on the spot, and took others out to be hanged. Dissatisfied by the slow pace with which one of their victims was strangling in the noose, they drew their pistols and made target practice on his body, twitching in the air. Peace returned to New Orleans.

Joe Hyland moved operations across the parish line to the foot of Monticello Street and started the Original Southport Inn. It catered to a clientele of socialites, politicians, and law enforcement personnel, except for those men in blue who were working off-duty shifts at the crap tables or the entry door. Hyland brought in two brothers as assistants, Rudy and George O'Dwyer. Everything in the gambling business depended on brothers, uncles, and other family members. You needed reliable backup. The O'Dwyer boys ended up owning the place, renaming it the Old Southport Club, and operated it into the 1940s when it burned to the ground. A lot of buildings burn in New Orleans. George then went up Monticello Street to open the New Forest Club.

Along the way, the O'Dwyers had won the ear and the protection of Governor Huey Long, then Earl Long, and a string of Jefferson Parish sheriffs, legislators, and police jurors who made token raids to maintain appearances and otherwise kept the business secure. Gambling was illegal, open, and thriving. As Rudy's grandson recently observed, they received communion every Sunday at the Mater Dolorosa mass. Rudy himself had paid for the church's magnificent stained-glass window. What more protection did you need?

Meanwhile, the Italian mob was rising again, this time in the form of Carlos Marcello, who was also based in Jefferson Parish. He had taken over from the Matrangas and was ready to expand. His big chance came from far-away New York City, where Mayor Fiorello LaGuardia had declared war on the mob ("Drive the bums out of town!") and seized their slot machines. New York crime boss Frank Costello hid his remaining slots and went looking for another venue. It soon came with an invitation from a United States senator from Louisiana, Huey Long.

By early 1935 Costello had at least a thousand machines in and around New Orleans. He set up his operation in the parishes through the Jefferson Music Company, owned by Carlos Marcello. When the Old Southport Club burned, Marcello built the New Southport and went on to operate the even more upscale Beverly Club inland from the river. All through World War II, gambling in Jefferson Parish remained illegal, mob run, and a welcome diversion for the troops passing through. As the O'Dwyers saw it, the clubs were providing a service. The New Orleans FBI office saw no evil as well, and heard no evil and reported no evil. Indeed, it reported no organized crime at all.

Life in the Free Parish of Jefferson, as it was called, all changed with a senator from Kentucky named Estes Kefauver, his committee counsel named Robert Kennedy, and a stool pigeon named Joe Valachi. Kefauver held public hearings on organized crime, and Valachi showed up with a bag over his head to protect his anonymity, although he had been identified and marked for death long before. Valachi's story of mob killings and political control staggered the Congress and the nation. The FBI could no longer deny the existence of the mob. Marcello was called to testify before the Kefauver Committee, and young Kennedy grilled him about his operations in Jefferson Parish. Marcello took the fifth a record 152 times. The only question he answered was whether he'd done anything illegal at all. "I wouldn't know," he replied, "I'm not a lawyer." He made Kennedy look foolish, which was a mistake.

The upshot of the Kefauver hearings was to drive Louisiana gambling back underground for a while. Not too underground, however. The O'Dwyers continued to run their operations out of the basement of the family home on Monticello Street and the back of yet another new club, O'Dwyer's, on Jefferson Avenue. Nothing very covert here. Marcello continued to operate the New Southport and Beverly through intermediaries. The governor had signed off, the sheriff had signed off, and that was all that was needed.

Until on May 26, 1953, the state police under a new governor raided the O'Dwyer home and found an "elaborately furnished" casino averaging a profit, not a take, of ten thousand dollars a night. In 1953 dollars. Members of the family ran across the street to their mother's house with the remaining cash. George was called. He rushed to the scene, got out of his car, and died of a heart attack on the driveway. It wasn't just the raid, his nephew explained. It was the feeling that the state had betrayed him.

Marcello's New Southport Club survived, down by the levee on the parish line. Good government came and went. In the late 1950s word came from the governor's office that if the O'Dwyers wanted to stay in the gambling business they would have to give a percentage to Marcello. They said no, and if the governor insisted on it they would blow the whistle on gambling in the parish instead, which they proceeded to do.

The feds never got Carlos Marcello, although they brought several cases against him. On one occasion, under the direction of Robert Kennedy, now the attorney general of the United States, immigration agents kidnapped him and sent him to Guatamala. Marcello was soon back in the country, humiliated and fuming. Rumor has it, and there is more than rumor, that Marcello never forgave the Kennedys, and that he had something done about it in Dallas in November 1963. That he met with his cohorts and discussed it now seems a matter of record, FBI record at the time. For whatever reason, the FBI never sounded the alarm.

The story does not end here. In another spasm of good government the Louisiana legislature proposed a new constitution in 1974 declaring that gambling "in any form" was illegal and would be "suppressed" by the state. Governor Edwin Edwards, however, was of a different mind about gambling and had the legislature formally approve it. An equally compliant state supreme court, despite the constitutional prohibition ("in any form"), upheld the legislation by concluding that the casinos were not engaged in gambling, but rather in "gaming." There is no challenge too great for the finely tuned legal mind.

I have a friend who gambled once at Southport when he was a kid, growing up at the foot of Carrollton Avenue near the batture.

He said that he put twenty cents together and bet them on the roulette wheel. He lost. They gave him seven cents for trolley fare as he went out the door. He kept the seven cents. He lived a short walk away.

MOLYTONES

"THERE'S NOT A MAN ALIVE can beat my molytones," says Alcide Verret over his gas stove. "I cooks them nine different ways."

We are standing in his tiny kitchen as he ladles out a serving of this strange fruit. Bayou Sorrel is running in the background, about a half mile from where it meets the Atchafalaya River and continues down to the Gulf of Mexico. The Atchafalaya used to be the Mississippi in its time, and would already be the Mississippi again if the threat of that recapture hadn't animated Congress to put a billion-dollar barrier upstream to hold the process back. Every year, though, it's a risk, and over a long enough period of time the Atchafalaya will win. In the meantime, here is Alcide on the Sorrel batture with a house the size of a carport and a garden as big as a ball field.

"They molytones," Alcide continues, "the man come out to get some and I said to him, you got to buy a *pair*." Blue eyes are twinkling under his thick gray hair. His hands and neck are reddened to the rim of the shirt, and from there the skin is entirely white. "The man said, 'A *pair*?' and I said, 'That's right. It's the onliest way they going to grow.'"

He picks two fresh fruits from a green vine by the doorway and shows me, head to tail. The tail end has a little point on it which he fingers gently. "That's the male," says Alcide.

I didn't see molytones again for a long while. I couldn't even find their name in the dictionary, and when I asked my mother-in-law, who cooked about anything, she said that she was stumped too.

I forgot about them until an afternoon, many years later, when I was walking on the levee by the Corps of Engineers and saw a vine crawling up the fence with wrinkled, green softballs hanging on it. I said to a fellow nearby that they looked familiar, and he said, "Merlitons," which does appear in the dictionary. Once you notice something you start seeing it everywhere, and, sure enough, the following week I came across the same vine clinging to the side of Campagno's restaurant just three blocks from the woods. I went inside and there they were on the menu, Alcide's molytones, deep fried and salted, which is enough to sell anything down here. We ordered them every time we went in.

Alcide and I now sit at his table. It is high noon outside. The life of the swamp does not fight the heat, it rises and falls with it, and so Alcide gets up early to run his fish traps, returns to hoe his garden, and maybe goes out in the evening after raccoons. Come noon he's in the shade. We are eating molytones two different ways and neither of them fried, which is a trick in itself because the insides of this fruit are gooey and near-tasteless. It takes a cook to fix them. I remember going fishing with Charlie Bosch, whose family goes back to the settlements at Des Allemands, and we got to his camp late and starving. Charlie pulled out some merlitons, tomato paste, onions, and a can of oysters, and by the light of a Coleman lantern he whipped up a dish that you would have paid a hundred dollars for at Arnaud's, easy. Cajun men do food.

"I could live away from the river," Alcide is saying while wiping his plate. "I could live in a big town, New Iberia, lots of places, wouldn't have to hit a lick at a snake." He looks at my bowl. "Here, have some more, don't you *like* my molytones?"

Alcide grew up on the banks of Bayou Chene across the main Atchafalaya. There used to be a town there nurtured by fishing and small crops on the ridges until the cypress boom. The logging changed life as dramatically as the oil boom would a half century later, sending the men deep into the swamps to cut down the tall trees, open routes to float them out, and sell them for the houses of the region. Swamp cypress boards have lasted for a hundred years, and could last a hundred more. Cypress wood does that. Alcide's daddy became a cypress logger. Alcide went out with him as soon as he was big enough to haul water and sharpen the saw. That is how he lost the rest of the family.

His mother kept two canisters outside the front door, one for cooking water and the other with kerosene to light the stove. One morning, probably in a hurry, probably sleepy, perhaps with a child on her hip, she confused the two canisters, put the kerosene on to boil and struck a match to light the stove. The explosion, says Alcide, shot her out of the house and shot part of the house into the bayou. The rest burned in minutes. He and his dad came in to find nobody left.

We go back to eating molytones. Alcide tells me that he knows the secret of Tabasco sauce, but he won't tell a soul. He motions to a large crock in the corner with a pile of rocks on the top. "Made of they hot banana peppers," he says. "No good man is going to eat one fresh." He smiles at a memory. "This boy Jerry, he say he *never* see a pepper he will not eat. Well, I give him one of my banana peppers and he could not finish it. He had to let it go." He smiles with satisfaction. "Jerry said, 'Why they is the *hottest* peppers I ever undertook.'" Alcide points again to the crock. "All kind of people tried and tried to find the Tabasco secret," he says. "And there it is."

Outside the door the insects are humming, the water is barely moving, and there is not another sound to break the air. I am thinking how lonely I would get out here. It is one thing to visit a place like this along the river, even to camp out for a couple of months, dodging the life beyond. But choosing to live here and making it work is another order of person. You find similar lives in Alaska or used to, before cell phones roped them in. The forgotten power of being able to be alone.

Alcide has read my mind. "Well don't you know," he tells me, "I go to town and pass three or four days and it is like the man *club* me." A pause. "All those smells in the *air*."

At the time I met Alcide there was only a handful of people living on riverbanks in the Atchafalaya swamp, one couple and three men getting on in years. To the best of my knowledge, none of them remains.

GHOSTS

They came with flashlights at an early morning hour when the parish was asleep. They entered the old plantation building and attached cables to the columns and another to the chimney inside. They ran the cables to a large bulldozer on the front lawn and were ready by dawn. Then they revved up the bulldozer and within minutes the 144-year-old Welham plantation was torn to the ground. As a finale they pulled a steel cable through the wreckage, reducing it to rubble. By the time the news photographers arrived, the deed was done.

Granted, they owned the plantation. Marathon Oil Corporation had bought it a few years before, with no intention of keeping it around. It was looking for an industrial site and this one sold cheap. For those same few years St. James Parish and the local historical society had been trying to persuade Marathon to put a caretaker inside to keep out vandals, to fix the roof, and to keep the building alive for another use. In fact, they thought they had an agreement that Welham would not be razed until an arrangement was worked out. At eight in the morning, upon hearing of the demolition, they sent an urgent telegram to Marathon asking it to stop. The telegram was never answered. A Marathon spokesman said later that the company was already helping to restore the San Francisco plantation downstream, and that saving one was enough. "We can't respond to every incident," he explained.

The blowback was fierce. State newspapers ran editorials with titles like "The Rape of Welham." Cartoons showed Marathon Oil handing General Sherman a bulldozer to finish his job. Legislators of both parties in Baton Rouge called it "sordid," "dastardly," and "a damn nasty thing to do," one suggesting that people who came down "from Ohio, New Jersey, and New York" to do things like this belonged in jail. A local resident said philosophically that she always "figured they'd do this at midnight." She was off by only a couple of hours. On May 5, 1979, before the start of a working day, the shrinking list of Louisiana's Great River homes went from ten to nine.

If you ride north on the levee top, the first plantation you see is Destrehan, just short of the spillway. On the river side the batture is wide and straight, and off your right shoulder is a set of live oak trees surrounding a deceptively simple dwelling. They came in all shapes and sizes, from the plain raised cottage to the majestic Nottoway, its second gallery looming like the prow of a ship, and the baroque San Francisco, whose gazebos and turrets painted yellow and blue look more like something from a putt-putt golf course. One hundred and fifty years earlier Mark Twain recorded the "great sugar plantation dwellings" that lined both sides of the river for long distances, cheek by jowl, and made the river "a sort of spacious street." The river was the road. Now the road is full of ghosts. You can guess where they used to be by the lines of live oak trees with arms like giant pythons. But there will be nothing at the end of them. And for the most part, the trees are gone too.

They shaded and sheltered the most beautiful death camps in the world. Of all the lives of the slaves in America, those on the Louisiana sugar plantations were the worst. Being "sold downriver" was close to fatal. The planters had started with any crop that would sell back home, but by the 1800s it was all about sugar, and growing sugar in the swamp was a machine with an insatiable appetite for bodies. In the early 1700s there were 5,000 slaves in the region. Within fifty years there were 20,000. By the start of the Civil War there were more than 330,000 and they all did sugar. Which then crashed. Before the war had ended the number of Louisiana sugar plantations had gone from 1,400 to fewer than 200. Many owners hung on as stubbornly as Scarlett O'Hara, but there came a starving point when pride could no longer prevail.

All along the batture, the plantations started to fall. People with money turned away from the river, which no longer took their crops to New Orleans, brought in their store goods, or delivered the mail. The modern towns formed inland along the railroads, and then the paved roads, and then the interstates, and that's where white people lived. The sons and daughters of the slaves, like survivors of a forest fire, moved cautiously out of the woods and swamps to the riverside, forming small communities. Some even came to occupy the big house. There is a photograph of the former Trapagnier plantation by the spillway, occupied to the hilt like the most crowded tenement building in Brooklyn, the once proud galleries draped with sheets and drying clothes. The back of town had come to the river, and it was living there when the next cataclysm arrived, the petroleum industry.

Petroleum needed the river to float its boats, cool its chemical plants, and carry away its wastes. Those liquids that they did not discharge directly into the Mississippi—it was a big river—or into the air—all folks knew was that the air smelled funny—they injected into the ground. They called their storage areas "tank farms." Within a few decades Louisiana had an entirely new plantation culture along the batture with remarkable similarities to the old one, 136 major facilities in 150 miles of river. The owners were even more remote from the day-to-day than they had been in the past; in this new world they were not even in Louisiana, and the impacts were left to the poor and the black who now lived there and to some extent worked there, although not many of them. As the plants went high-tech they employed fewer people, with greater skills, whom they brought in from the North.

Louisiana's understanding with the petrochemical industry was no secret. If the industry put plants here, the state would leave them alone. There were no unions and few labor laws. There were no environmental laws either, and when they finally arrived their enforcement got lost in the in-box. As an added inducement, the legislature exempted industry from local property taxes—the primary means in the river parishes for funding schools, health clinics, and libraries. Every ten years these exemptions from local taxes were renewed, no matter what the companies did to these communities in the meantime. Marathon Oil along with everyone else. Huff and puff about the razing of Welham plantation all they would, these same legislators welcomed Marathon and its sisters to the Mississippi River and handed over the keys.

A handful of plantations remain. They are some of the most beautiful structures ever erected in the American South, and they remain green oases in a sea of industrial and residential sprawl. For those with even minimal memory, they link us to our past. But what a reminder that past is, the horror in our closet. The owner of Laura plantation upstream bought three dozen young black women to breed slaves as a crop. Could anyone be blamed for wanting to bulldoze the last plantation, as we did the Reichstaag in Berlin? Swallowing hard, I end up thinking yes, they could. History talks. Or at least I want to believe that it does.

There are times when this belief is difficult. Visiting the Oak Alley plantation some years ago I heard a fellow in golf shorts say to his wife, "I got to build me one of these babies!" Of course, the owners of these plantations thought the same thing in their time. There are times, I confess, riding the levee by Destrehan or Ormand plantation I can imagine myself out on the veranda with a julep in my hand. The batture trees and the river are as pretty as they have always been. But off to the other side, what is it that we see?

RIVERMEN

You MIGHT SEE A COUPLE of them at the rail of the big tankers, thirty feet above the water, looking at the batture as they go by. They rarely wave back. They seem like distant prisoners on a traveling jail, serving out their time. The other day the paper reported that a couple of them had jumped ship just north of the city, swimming to shore. The sheriff's office was said to be looking.

They were a Chinese crew, apparently, on a ship owned by a Greek businessman, registered in Liberia, last inspected in Panama, piloted by an Armenian captain, picking up oil in Louisiana for a company in Japan, each of them a separate entity in the elaborate shell game of admiralty law that begins with "flags of convenience" and goes underground from there. Comes an accident, finding out who is liable can stump accountants and lawyers for years. I am not just looking at a big boat out there; I am looking at a floating triumph of legal artifice.

Whether they found the Chinese men I never found out, but the story seemed rather sad. I felt the same sadness when I came across a tugboat pilot in the woods shortly after Katrina, waiting for orders on his next cargo from someplace up in Tennessee. He was pleasantly drunk, his large white belly open to the breeze, and I could smell the urine around his resting spot near the boat, the *Sweet Miss Marie*. This is what had become of the rivermen of the Mississippi, no more legendary set of creatures in American history, half horse and half alligator, a bigger threat to public order

in the river towns than the river itself and the scourge of New Orleans. They were also the lifeblood of New Orleans for nearly fifty
formative years.

I can see them out there, riding the middle current where the
water is swift and hides fewer snags, the flatboat barges in all sizes,
slapped together back on the farm, and hoping to finish one long
journey with a load of whiskey, piglets, fabrics, or early corn, and
the sleeker keelboats, made to last and topped by slant-roofed cabins with sweep poles that ran their length like a boom. The crew
are in the open, lounging like hunting dogs, shooting dice, playing
cards, spinning yarns, and towards evening, the corn whiskey, the
sounds of whoops, and a song. I am trying to think of who, engaged in what occupation, still sings songs these days.

These boats were the first queens of the river trade and the early
months of 1801 recorded nearly five hundred flatboats, two dozen
keelboats, a brig, two schooners, and seven pirogues landing from
the north on the batture of New Orleans. But the kings of the trade
were the wild men who brought them down, manning the sweeps
and poles, dodging snags or a roiling log that could rip open the
hull in a heartbeat, navigating by brute force and the grace of a God
whose name they took in vain by the hour. It was not pretty country down here. The rolling hills above Natchez gave way to muddy
banks, quicksand, and invisible bars, an "inhospitable and impenetrable wilderness." This is before one describes the mosquitoes.
Few of the men could swim. It would not have made much difference. A historian of the period writes, "But to swim this thing!
To fight this cruel, invulnerable, resistless giant that went roaring
down the world with a huge, uprooted oak tree in its mouth for a
toothpick . . . this dare-devil boy-god that sauntered along with a
town in its pocket, and a steepled church under its arm for a moment's toy!" Many rivermen drowned, unrecorded. It was an event
as unremarkable as a cloudburst.

Wherever the rivermen landed, like their brother, the river, they
created a havoc of their own. It was a badge of honor. When a
boatman was arrested for a misdeed in Memphis, several hundred

others rose up together, set him free, and then shut down the town. In New Orleans, where constables were scarce, the rivermen faced little challenge except from their own ranks. Which, nonetheless, could be considerable. A song of their iconic hero, Mike Fink, begins with the boast that he was "half-alligator" and could "ride tornaders" and could "out-feather, out-jump, out-hop, out-skip, throw down and lick any man on the river." And he pretty much could.

Fink was a massive man who ruled the upper river with his prodigious strength and a habit of shooting tins of whiskey off the heads of his companions, except his lady companions, who held the tins between their knees. He is said to have picked off the warlock of an Indian chief who was standing on the riverbank as Fink's keelboat went by. Fink was brought low in his later years by drink and a young companion named Carpenter, for whom he held great affection, and whom he killed by accident when his aim wavered in a game of shoot-the-whiskey-cup. A spectator named Talbot killed Fink a few days later, following which, Talbot himself perished while trying to cross the river at high water in a skiff. This is before we get to the tall tales.

Dominating the New Orleans scene, however, was Annie Christmas, who carried a reported 250 pounds on her six-foot, eight-inch frame and a blond mustache that curled to the sides. In the Queen City known for deadly assault and waterfront mayhem, she topped the marquee in brawling and lovemaking, clawing, ear biting, eye gouging, and whoring with the best of both trades. She is said to have held competitions among other prostitutes for servicing the greatest number of men on a given evening, and usually won. It was also said that Annie, who sported a necklace of beads shaped like eyeballs for the men she had maimed, could walk a gangplank with a barrel of flour on her head and one more under each arm, which might well be true. It was also said that, when told by Mike Fink that she ought to be home mending socks instead, she lifted a bale of hay over her head and threw it into the Mississippi River with such a splash that it picked up Fink and carried him all the way to Natchez. That part might not be true.

The flatboats lined up along Tchoupitoulas Street, flank to flank, more than a thousand in a good year, and ashore of them lay a hellhole called simply the Swamp. There were no police. The dead might lie there for days. Names such as House Of Rest For Weary Boatmen and the Sure Enuff Hotel covered every vice desired, and for those that dared to spend the night only the vigilant survived. Discovering that the Sure Enuff had been leased out for gambling to a pair of Mexican brothers, Big Bill Sedley, the king of New Orleans riverboaters as undisputably as Annie Christmas was their queen, is said to have walked into the establishment armed only with a knife, locking the doors behind him. When the sounds of mayhem and breaking furniture abated, he threw open the doors to invite the crowd in for free drinks, stepping over the bodies of the Mexican brothers on the floor.

For the rivermen, attaining New Orleans was only half the journey. The trip back home was the most dangerous piece of all. The keelboats were poled north against killer currents by gangs of twenty men or more, or winched slowly from tree to tree. The flatboaters made the long trek by land, which could be even worse. En route they were marauded by pirates who created their own legends, among them the Harpe brothers who, along with three women companions, murdered scores of returning boatmen apparently for the pleasure of it. The competition among the predators was so keen that they took to placing signs on the bodies of their victims like calling cards: "Mason of the Woods." Perhaps the most ingenious of them was the notorious "Captain Plug," who would sign on with a flatboat crew and, on a predetermined evening, bore holes in its hull, allowing his criminal associates to row out to the floundering boat in skiffs, rescue Plug, skim off the cargo, and leave the rest of the crew to its fate. Plug is said to have met an untimely end when his associates were tardy in arriving, and he went down with the goods.

As I blink my eyes, the boatmen are gone, replaced by the paddle wheelers, then the steamers, then railroads, and, now, by another long tanker coming upstream, the nameplate reading *Petro Century*.

It carries an American flag on the conning tower, a flag of registry to the rear, perhaps Monrovia, its bright collection of colors obfuscating the fact that the country itself is little more than fiction and the ship's owner a post office box somewhere offshore. It is its own world. High up in the tower behind darkened windows like gigantic sunglasses is an individual surrounded by radar screens and gauge readings for the depth soundings, fuel levels, engine pressure, and the bilge pumps. There are no human beings in sight.

I am seeing two picture frames. One holds the Chinese crewmen who are probably hiding out in the woods upriver, frightened and alone, and my potbellied captain of the tugboat *Sweet Miss Marie*. In the other frame are their ancestors, the keelboaters, who were the batture's defining creatures, water and land, half alligator, half horse, and Look-At-Me! coming round the bend, and then gone so quickly, overtaken on the journey from whatever they were to wherever we are going. Upstream, the *Petro Century* angles west and disappears.

HIGH WIRES

It was late summer, the river was low, and several dogs were mauling each other happily in the shallows up by Ochsner Hospital. Every once in a while one would bound up the bank to where I was sitting, shove its wet fur into my side, look at me for appreciation, and then bound off again. I gave up any thought of reading and instead watched the sun drop behind the power plant across the river. The sky turned orange, a dead clear evening, strong breeze up from the south. That's when I heard the whistling ducks.

They were coming downriver in formations that seemed to shuffle like playing cards, their excited cries rising above the whine of boat motors and the plant across the way. They sounded like school kids out for recess, out for summer break, supercharged, they just couldn't wait to get there, wherever there might be. Then I saw them make their move.

There are two sets of high voltage lines that cross the river at this point, from the power plant to east bank transfer stations. Each set carries six thick wires like bars on a page of music, only these bars stretch for nearly a mile, over one hundred feet in the air. Approaching the wires the ducks made a sharp right turn, flapped hard, gained altitude, and then slid over the top of the lines like a high jumper, just clearing the bar. It was like watching ballet.

I was distracted for a moment by the dogs, but as I looked up again a bird in the back of a formation had just crumpled up in the sky, turned from ballet dancer to gunny sack in an instant, and then began plunging down towards the river, headfirst, neck extended in a grotesque way as if it were searching for something that it would never find. It hit the water with such a shock that I could hear it above the background noise. Then it disappeared. It did not float. It just disappeared.

I heard a voice say, "Holy Christ!" but when I looked there was nobody else around. It had to have been me. The dogs heard it, though, and paused ever so slightly at the edge of the water before resuming their play.

Everything had changed. This spot on the river, which had been my refuge from the day, suddenly seemed ominous. I looked at the next flights coming on with trepidation, invested now not in the beauty of their motion but in their dance with death. Several big lines made it up and over, not by much; they were fighting a south wind. Then came another group that I could see was in trouble because it had started too low to make the climb. It tried—the ducks were almost vertical with flapping wings, struggling to gain altitude, but in the end they simply faced into the grid, weaving through it like fish. Again, one struck, folded up in midair, tumbled forward, and began the long, seemingly endless plunge to the river. My guess is that it was already dead. I hope so. That is a lot of volts up there.

I started doing the math. I had been here for less than an hour and I had seen two birds go down. It is possible that the two I saw were the only ones downed that evening—I cannot prove otherwise—but it seems likely that there were more. This is a resident flock. The birds were running this transect every evening, up and down the river and past these lines.

How many of them die? Over a river, you'd never find the bodies. You can go to the literature, you can talk to the ornithologists, no one can give you a good number. The best guess of the U.S. Fish and Wildlife Service is that transmission lines kill from several hundred thousand to five million birds a year. That is quite a range, but this much seems established. The higher wires are worse, and the power lines by Ochsner are high. The ones near habitual flight routes are the worst, and the Mississippi is the biggest flyway in North America. The ones near wetlands are the worst, and New Orleans is surrounded by water. And the larger birds take the worst hit. Whistling ducks are large, the size of geese, with soft tan bodies, dapper black wings, white on the neck and legs, and beaks the color of red wine. That is a beautiful flying machine, going down.

The fish and wildlife people say that they are encouraging power companies to put little yellow balls on the lines. They say at least some birds seem to avoid them. But the whistling ducks fly in very low light. You can hear them passing over in the full dead of night. Some nights are cloudy and have no light at all. Adding electric lights to the lines might deflect them, or they might attract them. Another several million birds a year are drawn into illuminated city buildings and crash. They are swept up from the pavement early in the morning. It seems very hard for humans not to kill the creatures around them.

A black man in a suit and tie came over the levee to collect his dog. We stood together for a moment, looking out over the river. "Sure beats Chicago," he told me. I agreed and I knew it was true, although I'd never been there. I told him about the birds, and at that moment a large V of them materialized out of the gloom, shrieking as they flew. The wind had come up in their faces and they seemed disastrously low, would never make the climb. We watched them, together, not saying a word as they wheeled, tried to rise, too late, and were swept into the grid. My heart was in my throat. When the last one emerged from the other side, safe, I discovered that I hadn't been breathing.

The man turned to me, bright light in his eyes. "They made it!" he said.

CASINO

He is standing at the entrance of Audubon Park, facing the narrow road that loops around inside and has been off-limits to automobiles for years. At the present moment it carries a stream of joggers in all sizes, the lean and the pudgy, an evening ritual of uptown New Orleans passing him by. He is leaning on a cement balustrade in a sport shirt and slacks, silver hair combed to perfection. His face is inscrutable, but I am thinking how alien this scene must look to him. He is not in a city that loves him like the rest of the state loves him, and it is engaged in a physical activity here that he would not do himself at the point of a gun. He is the governor of Louisiana, and in a courtroom downtown he is on trial for racketeering.

The joggers keep on coming, their feet sounding like a slapping rain. Not one stops to say hello. He is the most powerful man in the state and he looks completely alone. Within a few years he will bring the "world's largest gambling casino" to Louisiana at the banks of the Mississippi River. It will be his legacy.

It had to seem unfair, the trial. Here he was returning to the governor's mansion after a cocky, one-sided campaign during which he accused his opponent of needing "an hour and a half to watch 60 Minutes," adding famously that the only thing that could defeat his return would be to catch him in bed "with a live boy or a dead girl." Only to be greeted by a federal indictment charging him with rigging state licenses to build hospitals, which, magically, had been granted to himself and were then sold to bona fide health care providers for a million dollars apiece.

The government's case fell apart when its witnesses, former Edwards appointees, suffered bad memory lapses on the stand, but the trial produced one sensational piece of news. It turned out that, perhaps with these hospital license proceeds, perhaps not, Edwin Edwards was regularly sneaking off to Las Vegas to gamble with the high rollers carrying paper bags of unmarked bills and signing the hotel register under such pseudonyms as "T-Lee" and "B-True." Uptown New Orleans, very much of the opposite political persuasion, had a field day. T-Lee! Who could make *that* up?

To which the governor would respond. Less than three hours after the jury failed to reach a verdict on the hospital cases, Edwards told the press that he had a plan to "revitalize" the state's economy. Three weeks later his plan emerged: casino gambling in New Orleans. The city that had mocked him about trips to Las Vegas was going to eat its words.

There is no doubt that Edwards believed in gambling. He also believed in the privileges of power. I happened to be invited to lunch with him one day while he was out of office, and he mentioned that the incumbent governor had apparently been ticketed for speeding over in Lake Charles. "Do you know what the man *did?*" he asked around the table. Nobody knew. "The man *paid* the ticket," he said, repeating it for emphasis "The man *paid* the ticket." The point was clear. What more proof of political incompetence did one need? In the end, it would take all the political competence Edwards could command to pull off the casino project. Then, with a terrible irony, it would bring him down.

The proposal I first heard about was over the top. One evening at a university function I ran into an Edwards supporter who, after assuring me that people around the state thought Edwards was "the messiah," laid out the grand plan. There would be only one casino in New Orleans, but the people who worked there would be recruited from all over the state and trained out in Crowley—the croupiers, the money managers, the girls with the drinks. Think of it, he told me, "an all-Louisiana enterprise." All I knew about Crowley was that Edwin Edwards was from there, throw in old cotton fields, patches of swamp, and a little sugarcane. It was about two towns west of Rayne, the Frog Capital of Louisiana, which was about two towns west of Opelousas, which was still an hour away from Baton Rouge and a solid three from New Orleans. It was closer to Texas. The logistics looked like fantasy. Just the sort of thing that New Orleans might bite on.

The opposition in New Orleans was not based on the morality of gambling, its economics, or even its ties to organized crime. In fact, as one radio talk show host assured his listeners, in Atlantic City "they did not permit violent crimes on natives"; instead, "they mugged the tourists." However comforting this prospect, what offended New Orleans with its oddball affection for its oddball past was the prospect of dropping a Vegas-style operation next to the historic French Quarter. A local architect described the proposed design as a parking garage topped with minarets. It would be enhanced by nightly fireworks and water displays with colored laser beams, probing the sky. Uptown New Orleans was not amused.

Time, then, for a casino developer to offer city officials a free trip to his Hawaii resort. Some marveled at the sights. "You would be taken to your room by a tram-driven boat," one enthused, "past wild game on islands." Others looked inside the casino and reported it to be "the most pitiful experience." "You ought to see the people," a senator said, "dazed robotoids." They file them off "like little herds of cattle," drive them down to "the great emporiums with plastic dolphins and such," and then they "send 'em back to the airport." Maybe Nevada needed something like that, he observed, because "God knows why anyone would go to Nevada." The casinos fit there and probably in Atlantic City as well, which, he concluded, "has deceased also." New Orleans remained skeptical.

Meanwhile, the action shifted to Baton Rouge, where Edwards allies had filed a bill authorizing a single land-based casino in the city of New Orleans. The roller coaster ride began smoothly enough, with the governor serenely removed, took a sharp dip when a constitutional amendment limiting the gambling to only one casino was defeated, tilted alarmingly when the New Orleans delegation, losing its monopoly on the action, abandoned the bill, jumped the rails as the house of representatives voted against it, and suddenly jumped back on again as the governor came off the sidelines and put on a dazzling show of arm-twisting, skullduggery, and personal persuasion. In June 1992, legislation authorizing the casino came to a final revote in the house. As the speaker of the house, an Edwards man, called for the tally, the lights on the electronic recording board flashed green and red—and then abruptly went out. The speaker quickly announced fifty-three votes in favor, one more than needed for passage. The process then turned to "chaos," with members "literally jumping from their seats to object," others rushing the podium to verify, or change, their votes. When a printout of the vote was released fifteen minutes later with a tangle of amended votes, circles, and arrows it looked, like a "bad football play gone haywire." A freshman representative put a sign on his desk reading, "Gee, Toto, I don't think we're in Kansas anymore." Baton Rouge had spoken.

Like an alluvial river, forever abandoning its oxbows and carving new ones, little in Louisiana takes a straight course. Ten major casino companies were bidding for the prize in New Orleans, and in the end the Hawaii-based Hemmeter corporation beat out Caesar's Palace, one dares not examine exactly how. At the same time, however, the legislature had also created a casino board to license each location in the state. Mystifyingly, a few months later the board issued its license not to Hemmeter but instead to a consortium of local businessmen who had in common that they were all friends of Edwin Edwards and tied into yet another casino giant, Harrah's. Pandemonium reigned. One venture held the lease and two others held the license. The *Times-Picayune* headline of the following morning, in type three inches tall, read "NOW WHAT?"

Now what was Governor Edwards, to the rescue. Reconciling his good friends in each of the camps, he urged them to join forces and split the pot three ways. Who knows, with Edwards involved perhaps the split was four ways. No southern river can be blocked for long. The banks are too soft, and there is simply too much flow.

The river rolled on. Sensing more gold in these hills, the legislature soon authorized a dozen more casinos across the state, these to be placed in boats on water, ostensibly to avoid competition with the world's largest in New Orleans. Several of the floating casinos ended up in New Orleans as well, only they never floated. They never left the dock. An inspection of the captains' daily logs revealed such explanations as "underwater obstructions," "fast currents," and "gentle winds," prompting local wits to speculate on such new excuses as "keys left in other pants." No one seemed to miss the floating part. The casinos were soon taking in many millions of dollars a month, overwhelmingly from the pockets of local residents, and sending it to out-of-state corporations, minus a small take for the state.

For his part, Edwin Edwards said he would never gamble in Louisiana, because when he won people would say that he was favored by the house. He didn't need that, he explained, he could win on his own.

Only, in the end, he didn't win. He lost everything. The lure of profit from the casino licenses proved irresistible, and in an operation hauntingly similar to his earlier hospital scheme, several licenses were granted by Edwards allies to corporations that, miraculously again, turned out to be Edwards himself, and then sold for fortunes to major casino companies. This time the racketeering charges stuck. The taped telephone conversations were too incriminating for even a New Orleans jury to dismiss. On one recording Edwards and his son were trying to figure out, between bursts of laughter, what to do with all the money they were pulling in. They decided to buy a tugboat. A very Louisiana idea.

SEAGULLS

"LOOK AT THE BABY SEAGULLS!" she says to us as we walk by. She is on top of the levee facing the woods, the small, neat houses of River Ridge behind her, looking out at a squadron of small birds that are bombing the ponded waters about fifteen feet below. "They are baby seagulls," she explains, when we do not immediately reply. We could be new here, and she will apparently be our guide.

The fact is, we do not reply because these are not baby seagulls. They are adult terns, tiny and natty as little fighter planes, and they are here because the floodwaters are receding, the fish are trapped in the pools left behind, and the birds are feasting the way they do around a shrinking water hole; it is a jubilee. Farther up the levee we can see a dozen ibis in a line at the water's edge, probing with their improbably long beaks into the soft muck for grubs and snails. Most of them are mottled, white and brown, juveniles on their way to adult, and seeing so many young is a good sign. Lisa calls them "the fellas." However polluted this place may be, it hasn't killed them yet.

Then I hear Lisa say the unpardonable. She says to the lady, "They are terns." I cringe. Lisa could as easily have said, "A seagull is not even a species, dummy!" for the effect it was bound to have. Our guide shot back immediately, as if defending her young, "They're baby seagulls. I've been watching them." I said quickly that she might be right. They certainly looked like baby seagulls from here.

I was not being a coward. My problem is that I come from a family of frequent correctors. I know they believed they were being helpful, but that did not blunt the nail. Back in grammar school my nemesis, Betty Ann Alger, who was also, curse the luck, my next-door neighbor, came over during a drawing exercise to tell me that the perfectly good sky that I was coloring above the house, a solid blue line at the top of the page, was not the way sky looked at all. "Here," she said, grabbing my crayon, "like this!" and she filled in the background with hazy blue swirls. She was, of course, quite correct. Hers was exactly the way the sky looked and my way was ridiculous, and I hated her for it. So as you can see, I am a little sensitive when it comes to correcting people. Lisa later said, "You'd have corrected me in a heartbeat if *I'd* have said seagull," and I said, "That's different." Although now I'm hard-pressed to say exactly how it is different.

What I really felt was that we should be cheering this lady on because she was maybe one in a thousand visitors to the batture who see birds at all. Instead they are hiking, biking, and tending the kids, and Lisa and I have done all this and more, but all of these activities draw the eyes down to the feet and you never see the other world.

Every summer night this city of the pink skies goes to bed by the river in a cacophony of laughing gulls, up high and wheeling towards the lake. Flights of egret and ibis make their way silently below them, downstream towards Audubon Park. Upstream, croaking and squawking, come the night heron to take up their posts like the changing of the guard. It is the best aerial show in town. Like the river itself they seem taken as background, a music we do not hear, or if we hear it we tune it out like the noise of traffic and the kitchen refrigerator. But this lady heard them, saw them, seagulls or no. I was on her side.

My favorites are the hawks. One day in the woods I was standing by with some friends of Ricky's at the winter campsite and I heard a tremendous splash behind my back and one of the guys said, "Holyshitaneagle!" and by the time I turned around the bird was up out of the water, a thin wedge of river between the barges and the land, with something flopping in its talons. It was the sort of shot you travel to Alaska to see. I have to say, it was not an eagle, but it was an osprey, another fish-hunting bird that we also all but eliminated with pesticides, and with its bold mask in black and white it is even more striking in flight. I hadn't seen an osprey on the river before, and I haven't since, but I will remember seeing this one as vivid as a sunrise, the same concentration of experience. I cannot tell you a single other thing that happened that day, or even that month, without going back to a calendar. But I can tell you everything about the osprey, even the drops of water falling back.

The batture seems to be a hawk sump, a place where they are safe to be and from which bold pairs go out to forage and even nest in the city. There is a pair in the trees at the foot of Carrollton, only a hundred yards from the levee, and there was another pair Lisa discovered up near her school. When the school lets out, a run of large vehicles originally built to haul farm equipment and troops to the battle front and now used to carry a child or two lines up around three square blocks for the pickup. Lisa's assignment is to man one of the traffic posts on the far perimeter, under the live oaks, and that is where she first spotted the hawks. They were building a nest. She pointed them out to the drivers who, trapped behind their windshields, had nothing better to look at. Within a few days they were hooked. "How the hawks doing?" they would ask, using as few verbs as possible as we do down here. Lisa reported on their progress, the completed nest, the female on the eggs, the hatch, the fledging, at which point some of the drivers got out of their cars to look, and nobody behind complained. It was a happening.

A former student of mine lives on that same street, and when I told her about the carpool hawks she was cautious. There was a lady nearby who was scared to death of the hawks, she said. The lady had asked if it was legal to shoot them. She thought they would take her cat. I, too, have a neighbor, and this one is afraid of an opossum that comes in at night to climb up on the shed. They carry rabies, my neighbor told me, and though I said the record of kids getting bit by opossums is probably quite small, I could see I was making no dent here. We want to have nature around so long as it is safely not around.

This spring the hawks came back. They lit up the carpool with their buzz for about two weeks. Then they disappeared. I got a call from my friend on the street who said she found two dead hawks in her front yard. She thinks they were poisoned. I said, you could check it out, but she said, no, she'd already buried them in the woods. "Besides," she added, "what's the point?"

I could not answer the question.

JOE LOUIS

JOE LOUIS is telling me about the slate fights. "Wind blew them off the roof," he says. "We'd get a bunch and stand at the end of the street yelling to the kids on the next block." Then the missiles started to fly. "You could curve them, you know," he demonstrates, his wrinkled hands twisting in the air, "make 'em go left and right, sneak up on you sideways." He got hit in the eye once and shows me his scar, a small ridge of white against black skin. I show him my scar, cut right through my eyebrow. Throwing dirt bombs, I tell him.

Joe Louis grew up by the levee on General Ogden at the parish line, a street so derelict one end has no pavement still, and the houses look like river shanties moved inland a block and left askew. "It's a bad place, man," he says, shaking his head, "but we had some times." He starts telling me about making popguns from the chinaberry trees, and I find myself torn between two worlds, the familiar adventure of our childhoods and the fact that he is black and didn't grow up like me in northern New Jersey but along the Mississippi River before the days of integration and not long after the time you could find the dead bodies of black Americans swinging from the batture trees.

"You got to find yourself a piece of cane," he is telling me, "because they are hollow and just the chinaberry size." But I am still in no-man's-land here, stuck on the fact that he is telling me my own story, only we used tubes from vacuum cleaners and shot out soda cartridges we took from the trash bin behind Pride's Drug and

Fountain, he growing up black on the batture of New Orleans, the horror show of the American South. I don't know what I expected; I saw kids playing all over Korea at the end of the war there, carefree games in shot-up towns and fields still occupied by rusting military vehicles, but slavery down here was different. For one thing, it went on for 250 years.

I am listening to Joe Louis explain his trigger mechanism, which was quite ingenious. It popped a load of chinaberries from where we are sitting to, he searches for a marker, that drum out there, pointing to a floater which has come down river and swept into the eddy, revolving around and around as if having its own discussion about whether to come ashore or ride on towards the Gulf. But my mind is on the slave auctions, which migrated en masse to New Orleans after Congress finally shut down the import business in the early 1800s. The traffic continued, of course, on ships carrying contraband from the Caribbean—slaves were Jean Lafitte's stock-in-trade—and on wagons and barges from the north, slaves and the children of slaves brought in for lawful sale in the lobby of the St. Charles Hotel and on the scaffolds of a dozen open markets in town. They were also available, like prostitutes or a good horse, from every bartender and hotel concierge. The lion's share of the nation's slave trade, just the recorded trade, was transacted on the streets, squares, and back alleys of New Orleans. The risks were obvious.

The South's ultimate nightmare erupted just north of here, along the Mississippi, in 1811. The signals had been coming in for several years. In October 1804 Governor Claiborne received word of an "insurrection conspiracy" in Natchitoches, implicating thirty slaves and alleged Spanish and Indian instigators, which served to explain the phenomenon. To right-thinking people of the day, it would not occur to slaves to rebel on their own; theirs was a peaceable kingdom. Two months later the governor sent troops to quell "a spirit of insurrection" in Pointe Coupee Parish, uneasily closer to New Orleans. Twenty-three blacks involved were put onto a flatboat that floated south, stopping at each riverside town to hang one from a tree. The following year a slave plot was discovered in New Orleans itself, reportedly aimed at killing all local officials and declaring home rule. Toussaint L'Ouverture and the revolution in Haiti hung over the region like a pall. Then, in January of 1811, it happened on the Mississippi batture about thirty miles upriver from the Queen City and came marching south, in the words of one white observer, "a miniature representation of the horrors of Santo Domingo." It would be the largest slave rebellion in American history.

Joe Louis goes on to tell me about the chinaberry tree. Couldn't eat those fruits, he says, but you could shoot them from a slingshot a country mile. I haven't heard that expression for decades. I tell him that I'd owned the best slingshot in town, because the others used rubber from bicycle tires, but I had found some surgical tubes that stretched like garters and could put a rock through a cardboard box. It carried the initials of my girlfriend carved into the handle, MEL, only I had stuck the slingshot into my back pocket one afternoon when I went to see a parade, and a policeman took it away from me. Just like that. I still feel the injustice of it all. Joe Louis says that if he saw a kid with a slingshot today he'd start running the other way. Back in the day, we just popped bottles. We lined them up behind the garage, the old Coke bottles thick as sea ice and if you dropped them on concrete they almost bounced. They were the soldiers of Hitler's army and hard to topple. "These days," Joe Louis says, "the kids will kill you."

The slave insurrection was short and bloody. A mulatto named Charles, allegedly from Santo Domingo—which would satisfactorily explain his attitude—rose on Colonel Andry's plantation in St. Charles Parish, killed the son, wounded the father, and then linked up with slaves from other plantations and runaways hiding in the canebrakes along the batture. Things went well enough on the first day, moving downriver, until they arrived at the Fortier plantation, where they got into "killing poultry, cooking, drinking, and rioting," which seemed to have slowed them down. As their rumor spread, white families up and down the German Coast threw what they had into carriages and began pouring into the city.

On day two the white militia arrived, about eighty strong, to face about twice that number of blacks, only the militiamen were armed with shotguns and rifles instead of clubs and hoes. The slaves held their ground for a while, "colors displayed and full of arrogance" went the report, until the slaughter became too great and they broke for the woods and the shelter of night. By day three the U.S. Army had arrived on the scene, joined by companies of dragoons and artillery from Baton Rouge, and it was all over but the mopping up, "an open season on blacks in the vicinity."

Joe Louis says to me, after I tell him about the police taking my slingshot, that he used to be a policeman here in the city. I am thinking, a black policeman in New Orleans in the 1960s, which was just a few years before a police riot in Algiers so wild it caused the chief to resign. It must have been an interesting time, I say, neutral as I can. "I wasn't a bad cop," he tells me, in a way that also tells me that he wasn't exactly an exemplary cop either. I wait for him to go on. It seems that one night he and his partner found a brother with some drugs. "Wasn't so bad then, the heroin," he explains. "They'd just go off and sleep. Not like the crackheads today." There was a half year's salary for the two of them, right on the sidewalk. "I said to the man, 'Do you want to go with us, or do you just want to go away?'" Joe Louis continues, "I give him the choice, you see." The man went away. I scratch the sand and check out my dog, still lying apart in her own world.

"I used to prosecute drug cases," I say, "up in D.C." Joe Louis gives me a mock recoil, as if I had launched a punch. "Did it for several years," I continue, "but no matter who went to jail the street price never changed." I say, "I thought those guys were the scourge of the earth," but it is in the past tense, a life I no longer lead. I have come to a different view of who is really scourging the earth these days. The big drum finally spins out of the eddy and starts off downstream.

The white troops killed about seventy of the rebellious slaves and captured the rest, who were put on trial two days later. The result, of course, was never in doubt. The motives were of interest, though, and one slave, when asked, said simply, "Detruir le Blanc." There were no outside agitators. They just hated the white man and his system. For those who believed in the peaceable kingdom, this was a terrible message. The lid would not stay on. Twenty-one of the captured blacks were convicted and shot to death. The corpses were then decapitated and their heads placed on poles along the river, up and down the German Coast, to instruct "all who would disturb the public tranquility in the future."

On Christmas Eve, 1811, the governor warned local residents of a new "disposition to rise in insurrection" along the same plantations. Whites flocked to the city again. There were no more slave revolts along the lower Mississippi, but no one lived in tranquility either.

Joe Louis used to play up in the hobo jungle, along the railroad as it split from the river in Jefferson Parish through a stretch of old rosacane. It was thick in there and they had their paths, just right for the chinaberry wars. I tell him about the apple wars from the top of Crescent Hill. You cut willow sticks about three feet long, whippy as a dog's tail, stuck an apple on one end, tight enough to hold, loose enough to fly, and you could throw them all the way down to the road below and onto the roof of Mary Ellen List's house, whom I once saw crawl stark naked out of the shower at her brother's command to retrieve a softball we had banged into the gutter. I was in love with her from then on. "Yes indeed!" says Joe Louis, enjoying the picture. I do not spoil it for him by adding that we were both about ten years old.

Joe Louis and I are not friends. I only met him up here this evening, and I may never see him again. I don't know what to do with the closeness I feel with him over the chinaberry popguns and the rosacane wars, the joys of unsupervised space, a deep feeling, not like a movie we saw, something instead we went out and did. But I have a hard time wrapping my mind around being a black boy, in this town, in this area of town, at that time, and being happy. Of course, I tell myself, kids always play, in and around disasters, but this was a different kind of disaster. I cannot put myself into this movie. When I try, it always turns out badly. I end up hanging from a tree.

KATRINA

DIARY ENTRIES, 2004:

Tuesday, August 30: It is Tuesday afternoon and we don't know a thing. The storm has blown through, some trees are down, poles, wires, pieces of roof. The only station we can get on the radio is a call-in and they begin, Oh Jerry, I've Always Loved Your Show and then they say something about water coming up to the front steps. I go stand outside. A couple comes down the street with plastic bags in both hands, full of clothes, picking their way over the branches. I say, just making conversation, where's the water? He says, about four blocks up. Then she says, and there's a body in it, shot through the head. Then he says, and they ain't coming to pick him up. I say to my wife, ok, you win, I think we'd better go.

Saturday, August 27: I am in the checkout line at the Rite Aid buying flashlight batteries and last minute stuff. The guy ahead of me has a huge bag, getting ready for Katrina, he says. He empties the bag on the counter, one by one. A fifth of Jim Beam. Another fifth of Jim Beam.

Sunday, August 28: I get a call from a reporter on public radio. You're still there, he says. I say, yes. He says, will you talk with us about the storm when it comes? I say, ok. Later his producer calls back. She says, why are you there? Haven't you been writing for years about how bad these things are? I try to think of an answer. She says, you still on the line? I say, this is going to be a difficult interview.

Monday morning, August 29: The storm has made land. The house is shaking and it is pitch dark outside. The phone rings, thirteen times. Then it starts again. It is probably public radio. I have still not come up with an answer.

Monday evening, August 29: We get a call from our younger boy. The land line still works. He is out in California, glued to the television. We know absolutely nothing. He says, get out, the levee has broken. I say, take it easy. I say, when the Corps builds levees, they don't fall down.

Tuesday evening, August 30: We are driving down Freret Street and over the bridge, on our way towards Baton Rouge. Curious, some people on the bridge are carrying clothing and hauling children back into the city. Why would they be doing that? We don't know about them getting turned back on the other side. We don't know a thing. We find a radio station and it is saying that people with boats are being asked to come to the I-10/I-12 split. We pass some pickups hauling boats, coming the other way. I think, damn, I have a fourteen-foot flatboat in the backyard with a 15-hp motor, carries three, maybe four kids. People were stranded on their roofs and my boat was in the backyard.

Tuesday, September 6: We left the cat. Couldn't find it. Didn't even think to leave food behind. Just fled. Lisa tells our friend Charlie up in Mississippi that she misses the cat. Then we move on north. A week later we get a phone call. Ollie, he says, we are going in. I say, why? He says, to get your cat. I say, you'll get arrested and there aren't any courts. They'll send you to Guantanamo. He says, I got a badge and the AK-47. True, about the gun, anyway; I'd seen it spraying the grass on his country lawn. Last night we got another phone call. Ollie, Charlie says, put Lisa on. She takes the phone. I hear a faint meow. Lisa starts crying.

Wednesday September 7: We have landed in Virginia, a town called Crozet, maybe three hundred people with a single diner and a single waiter. We say, we're from Katrina. He says, did you see the president on television? We say, we didn't. Oh my yes, he says, the president said that he was asking everybody to pray for those people in New Orleans and I said right back to him, Mr. President, those people don't want you to pray for them, they want you to get them off their fucking roofs!

Monday, September 12: We say, we're from New Orleans and they won't charge us for the shirt. We ask directions and the fellow comes out with a map and marks the route on it. Then he gives us the map. We are walking on the towpath near Washington, D.C., and Lisa has a shirt that says New Orleans and we pass a couple, middle-age-plus, and they say, are you from New Orleans, and we say, yes, and they say, do you need a place to stay? Everywhere we go.

Thursday, September 22: The cat lost all of its hair. Probably hadn't eaten in a week. Charlie and his friends nursed it back to health on warm milk. It ended up sleeping on the family bed, up by the pillows. Got its hair back. Got fat. Walked out into the street one day and got run over by a truck.

Wednesday, October 5: When we drove out through Mississippi, it looked like it had been cut by a lawnmower with blades about forty miles wide. But as we drive back into New Orleans, it looks like Hiroshima. There are no street lights. We stop at a stop sign. The other guy is already stopped. I wave him forward. Then it's my turn. A woman waves me forward. It is the new drill. We are actually looking at each other, making eye contact, giving way. Maybe this is the end. Maybe this is the beginning.

Monday, October 10: So, how'd you do? The guy who is asking me lost everything and his family is somewhere in Oklahoma. The only people I see around are Mexican roofers and the national guard. Out in Gentilly, there are two guys throwing destroyed stuff out of their living room window. Wallboard, a mattress, woman's underclothing. The water line's at the roof. They are the only people for ten blocks. I go in. The refrigerator magnets hold kids' homework assignments.

Monday, October 24: I meet this fellow who did time in Angola. Lives in Mid City and the high water put him on the roof. Police came by in a boat but they wouldn't take his dog, so he refused to go. Came by the next day, same thing. Came by the third day and said, ok, bring the dog, and they took both of them to a ramp off I-10 and left.

Tuesday, October 25: I am talking with a guy who does roofs now. Used to do something else. Has a place on Esplanade with one of those Spanish roofs, all curved tiles. Goes up to check it after the storm. A helicopter spots him and comes over. The prop wash begins to lift the tiles. He waves the helicopter away. They think he is waving for help and come right on down. Blow away half his roof.

Tuesday, November 8: There were 485,000 people in New Orleans. I am doing a little calculus. Say each one has five Katrina stories. That's a million and a half Katrina stories. Like I say, we don't know a thing.

RABBIT

THE RABBIT CAME BARRELING UP THE SLOPE and across the path ahead of me like a racing dog, stretched flat out, ears laid back, one big eye showing white all around. The belly was swinging heavily; it could have been carrying young.

Then I saw the men. The one in the lead was coming up the same slope fast, yelling, "I got him! I got him!" and waving what looked like a club. It *was* a club, a golf club with a round wooden head, the kind that knocks the ball a hundred and fifty yards from the tee. Behind him was his son, couldn't mistake him for anyone else, a carbon copy of his dad halved to about three feet high and two feet wide, a little more cautious about the guy in the helmet he was seeing ahead of him, up on the levee top, on a bicycle, that would be me.

I braked hard and rose up on the pedals, curious, a question written all over my face. "Rabbit hunting!" the man said, waving his golf club. His eyes were as wide as those of the rabbit and his face flushed in the climax of the hunt. The rabbit was getting on down the far slope. This guy on a bicycle was in the way.

Doing the same calculus in my head, I slowed the bike to a crawl, looking beyond the two on the cement apron of the levee to the woods below, where another man and another boy were emerging from a bramble thicket set in shallow water. The man was wearing rubber waders, waist high, and had his own golf club in hand, its metal head set at an angle to blast shots out of a sand trap. His boy was carrying a stick.

There wasn't much space down there for rabbits that month. The Mississippi River had been at flood stage for a long time, leaving small patches of the higher ground for cover. Every creature that lived on dry land was compacted onto that space. From a hunting rabbits point of view, this was heaven.

I tried to digest the scene. By coincidence, although it was late afternoon, prime getting outside time, there was no one else in sight. What would these men have done if a family had been walking by? What would they have done if *I* hadn't happened by on a bicycle? Beaten the animal to death on the levee top? Stun it and then turn the clubs over to the boys, the way a good mother lion teaches her young?

I pedaled away, not looking back. I didn't want to know what came next. The yards down to my right were fenced off with chain-link mesh or wooden slats, the lawns mowed neatly to the edge, no bushes, not many spots for a rabbit to hide. Whether the hunting party pursued this one I cannot say.

Instead I began asking myself why I was so shocked by the spectacle. After all, humans have been chasing after animals in the wild since long before they were doing almost anything else. Like it or not, this was a very ancient play and, in its way, a very natural one. I wondered whether I would have reacted any differently had the men carried guns and were shooting at rabbits instead. I'm told the levee police do it from time to time.

Maybe it was the golf clubs. I never had the patience for golf, but it has always seemed an innocent way for mostly men to get away from mostly their wives and have something else to compete over besides making money. The settings of a golf course are also genteel, if deceivingly so, with the green grass, white clubhouse, and bright little vehicles so that you do not have to strain yourself by walking. Indeed I had just passed a golf course down the levee not half a mile away. Wielding golf clubs against a rabbit seemed a little like gents in tuxedos chasing after animals with their cutlery. It was the juxtaposition of it all.

The men after the rabbit were not in tuxedos, however. They probably lived in one of the tidy little houses below, with a plastic wading pool outside. I'll confess that I shot at sparrows, tin cans, bottles, and anything else we found in the woods when I was young. I had a .22 caliber rifle that a neighbor gave me when I had gone over the front of my bicycle and broken my nose, both wrists, and four front teeth. He came into my bedroom the next day and laid this sleek, deadly thing on the chair and said I want you to have this, and I forgot about the pain for a moment because I was receiving the gift of God. So I can get the idea of hunting, especially for kids. I only lost it when I grew older and saw more dead things.

On the other hand, hunting rabbits with clubs had something dark about it. I thought about the last page of Shirley Jackson's "The Lottery," when you finally realize that the good citizens of the town, in conformance with a ritual that extended back beyond memory, were beginning to stone one of their own to death. Then there are the snake roundups in Texas, everyone out in pickups dragging chains and on foot scouring the bushes until they've collected a writhing mass of panicked invertebrates, some harmless, some not, and then the fun begins, wading in with poles to put them in sacks and beat them to death. Maybe they just run over them with vehicles these days; I haven't stayed in touch. The question for me is what this kind of ritual does to the human soul. Is there any connection between being one of the few countries in the world that does these things for sport and one of the few still putting criminals to death?

But there are more layers here. The horse set in America and England still rides to the hunt, which means chasing a fox across the countryside until your dogs find it and tear it apart. Some folks in the west, I've been with them, think nothing of going out to shoot the heads off of a few gophers before breakfast. I have a friend in Mississippi who told me he was going over to the game farm in a couple of weeks to shoot his deer, because he hadn't gotten one when the season was open. I said I didn't know they grew deer on farms, and he told me they raised a kind of red deer from the British Isles just down the road, kept them behind a tall fence and fed them at stations. All you had to do was pay the fee, go sit by a feeding station, and wait. They had benches for you so didn't have to sit on the ground.

Some time later I read about the ill-fated expedition of the vice president of the United States, who accidentally shot his friend while hunting quail, which can happen to anyone. What struck me about the story, however, was that the quail had been kept in cages, and a guide for the party went out to the field with them, minutes ahead of time, and released the birds by hand. They were released upside down to disorient them, which would make them easier to shoot.

So where does chasing rabbits on the batture with golf clubs fit on this spectrum? My guess is that the men I saw might not have the air fare for a trip to the quail farm, although I think it was also reported that the vice president flew down free on a military plane. So do they not get their chance, too?

Truth be told, there are a lot of rabbits down on the batture along the Mississippi River. They would have to be quite numerous for my dog, who is pushing twelve years old now and has the eyesight of a potato, to find them. They are not going rare and endangered any time soon. On my return trip that evening I counted six big ones along the woods, out in the open and feeding. And yet, if they had started bolting up towards me again while out of the brambles came men and boys brandishing golf clubs and yelling, "I got him!" I think my reaction would still be the same. Thinking about things does not necessarily resolve them.

At the spot on the levee path where I'd seen the rabbit hunt, they were no longer in view. Instead, there were three teenage girls, two in school shirts and walking shorts, the third in a party dress. They were talking animatedly and not looking towards the woods at all.

1

LIBERTY

THE MOVIE IS IN BLACK AND WHITE. The opening shot pans slowly across the batture, past a tall monument, to the streetcars that circle deferentially around it, and then to Blanche DuBois who, in a southern voice tinged with decay, recites what a local writer calls Tennessee Williams's brilliant metaphorical question: "First you take a streetcar named Desire . . . transfer to Cemeteries . . . get off at Elysian Fields." There is no need to tell the audience anything else; we are in New Orleans. The trolleys, the river, and the voice, we could be in no other place in the world.

Except for the monument, a very ordinary column stuck in a tier of concrete. There is not a shred of art about it. No horseman sits on top of it waving his sword, no pilgrim steps onto new land. We could be in Indianapolis. And yet, it commands the scene. One hundred years earlier, under a hot September sun, with Abraham Lincoln dead for less than a decade, three and a half thousand men of the White League, commanded by former Confederate army officers, clashed nearby with an equal number of ill-trained and largely black militia, routed them, and installed an all-white government of their own. Thirty-two people died, only three on the White League side. It was a victory worth commemorating in stone.

The spot was ideal. The Liberty Monument rises at the fulcrum of the city, where Canal Street meets the Mississippi River, where the rafts and keelboats came to shore from as far away as Illinois and Ohio, where the big steamers that replaced them lined in a single wall of stacks and wheels, where the trolley lines turned, a green sward reached inland to separate the French Quarter from the American district, and a string of New York–class department stores began their run uptown, and where Rex, King of Carnival, would arrive each Mardi Gras to greet his subjects with doubloons. Here is the junction of America's largest artery of commerce with the New Orleans version of Broadway, Hollywood Boulevard, and the Champs-Élysée. Where Canal Street meets the Mississippi, you can feel the heart beating under your feet.

One hundred and thirty-five years after the White League insurrection, with all that has transpired in between, the monument here is still with us. Well, not precisely. No one is entirely happy with its fate. Then again, we can be thankful that nobody has shot anybody here for political reasons in a while. Not, of course, that they haven't wanted to. You can feel this heartbeat, too; it comes and goes.

No state in the South took to Reconstruction kindly, but Louisiana was a case apart. In 1873, a white paramilitary force attacked an all-Negro militia in northern Louisiana, killing some one hundred blacks in the process. Nearly half of them were murdered after they had surrendered. Later that year a like-minded band forced six Republican officeholders to resign and then assassinated them, along with five freed slaves who were witnesses. These successes led to a new organization, the White League, which, while the Klu Klux Klan was rising in the dark, was rising in the open. It listed its members in the newspapers. It held drills in parks and patrolled the city streets. It published a platform averting to the "supreme danger" of a "Christianity menaced by stupid Africanization." In the elections of August 1874, its armed squads camped next to the voting stations and obtained, depending on who was counting the ballots, either a victory or a close defeat for the governorship, then housed in the French Quarter.

Both sides thought the election had been stolen. The White League proclaimed, with haunting echoes forward, that it had sought only to "eliminate from the electorate the mass of corrupt and illiterate voters" that had "degraded our politics." Doubtless there was corruption and to be sure the black electorate was largely illiterate. Doubtless as well, although one will hear it denied, the league was more motivated by the specter of "Africanization" than it was by Athenian notions of good government. As it turned out, White League troops at polling places kept many blacks from casting ballots. Ballots in those days were printed on paper the color of the candidate's party, eliminating any possibility of secrecy. Recently freed slaves might have been unschooled but they weren't into committing suicide.

The federal government claimed foul, declared the Republican candidate the victor, and then, adding more insult to injury, proceeded to split political offices equally between the two races. It was too much to tolerate. The White League of New Orleans ordered a shipment of guns. The government proposed to confiscate it. We were at Lexington and Concord all over again.

On September 13, 1874, two weeks following the elections, a New Orleans newspaper published an announcement to its readers signed by over forty leading citizens that began, "For nearly two years you have been the silent but indignant sufferers of outrage after outrage heaped upon you by an usurping government." The Republicans, it was felt, after warping the Constitution to grant black people the right to vote, were now trampling on the Second Amendment's right to bear arms. "We therefore call upon you," the notice concluded, "to assemble at the Clay Statue on Canal Street" and "DECLARE THAT YOU ARE OF RIGHT OUT TO BE AND MEAN TO BE, FREE!" It was all about liberty.

The predicable followed. The league drew a large and angry crowd. The federal militia arrived and ordered them to disperse. Who fired first is probably irrelevant, and certainly not provable. The battle itself was brief. White League forces led by experienced Confederate army veterans outflanked the militia, who after a few volleys broke and ran. The governor's quarters were taken without incident, and thus, according to one account, "the Usurper and his supporters escaped the wrath of a victorious population." Not for very long. Despite boasts that the president would have to send down ships to evacuate stranded northerners, Ulysses S. Grant sent in more troops instead, the League backed down, and the Republican governor was put back in his mansion.

Not for very long. The federal appetite for enforcing civil rights in a hostile land was waning, and within a few years white supremacists had taken over the state, elected a White League governor, revived the old Black Codes of the slavery days, and sent Louisiana on a long slide into its own special darkness. Within which, the league's victory shone a bright light. At a first anniversary celebration of the event, a local leader declared with a sensibility particular to New Orleans that if the league was in fact a "mob," then it was "at worst a mob of gentlemen."

Unfortunately for New Orleans, its record in the Civil War provided few bragging rights. Tied to the North by the river and its commerce, the city was a conflicted ally to the case of secession and surrendered soon after the federal fleet went by. Then it turned to the lucrative trade of supplying the enemy. Here, however, was a history worth telling, stalwart whites defeating the northern invaders and their black allies. In 1888 the site was officially named Liberty Square. Three years later a monument appeared with an honor role at the base listing White League casualties. No mention was made at the time of the Republican enemy, an oversight that was corrected in 1934 with the addition of chiseled engravings explaining, on one side of the base, that subsequent elections threw out the "usurpers" and "gave us our state," and on the other side that new leadership replaced "Governor Kellog (white) and Lt. Gov. Antoine (colored)," the shame of which spoke for itself. Here the inscriptions remained chiseled into the base of the monument at the foot of Canal Street where it meets the Mississippi River, the beating heart of the city of New Orleans and passed by thousands of local commuters, tourists, and business visitors every day.

None of this appeared faintly anomalous to the city or, for that matter, its visitors until the civil rights movement produced black political leadership in New Orleans, and another Louisiana phenomenon, Klan leader David Duke. The Liberty Monument became their battleground. Black activists began mounting demonstrations at Liberty Square. In 1974, the centennial of the White League skirmish, the NAACP held its national convention at the adjacent Rivergate Center and called on the city to tear the monument down. These same protests catapulted Duke from little-attended debates on the LSU campus to firebrand rallies with fellow Klansmen in Liberty Square. What, he delighted his followers by asking, were we to do with the nearby statue of Andrew Jackson, replace it with "Stevie Wonder Square"? He struck a deep chord. In a later run for the governorship against the flamboyantly corrupt Edwin Edwards, Duke's chances of winning seemed so great that his opponents produced bumper stickers reading, "Vote For The Crook, It's Important!" The famous bumper sticker notwithstanding, Duke won the white vote. It was the black vote that elected Edwards, who continued to skate at the law's thin edge until he finally fell through.

Meanwhile, the city was torn over the Liberty Monument. Mayor Moon Landrieu, the last of the city's white mayors, had the league's inscriptions at the foot of the monument covered up, adding a bronze plaque which stated that "the sentiments expressed" were "contrary to the philosophy and beliefs of present New Orleans." He was partially right. But the covers were soon torn off to reveal the original inscriptions, and both sides began trading insults with graffiti, none of them scenic attractions. One read in all caps, FUCK OFF NAZI SCUM. The philosophy and beliefs of New Orleans remained badly split.

And so began a slow, New Orleans dance between the old and the new. The city's first black mayor, Ernest Morial, tried to remove the monument, only to be blocked by a white majority on the city council. In the late 1980s Morial's successor took a more subtle tack, removing the offending obelisk temporarily during wholesale reconstruction along the riverfront. He stuck it in a warehouse, where he apparently hoped everyone would forget about it. White sensibilities did not forget. Fearing that temporary exile was turning into permanent, a local druggist filed a lawsuit to rescue the monument from obscurity. His claim, joined improvidently by the New Orleans preservation community in a tactical blunder that marks them with the black community to this day, was that the monument was protected by law as a historic site. Which, in fact, it was.

The monument's fate, then, would turn on the views of the curators of state history, and the courts. To the black community, the monument was a symbol of racism, pure and simple. To a white lawyer at the time, it commemorated "righteous citizens recovering their government from an ignorant and corrupt administration." Judge John Minor Wisdom of the federal appeals court in New Orleans, whose ancestor had fought with the league, opined that the "big issue" was more "restoration of home rule and democracy." The White League could not have put it better. Then again, Wisdom's court went on to mandate the racial integration of LSU, department by department, then Louisiana secondary schools, transportation systems, and all public services down to bowling alleys and hamburger stands. White Leaguers were not happy with it. New Orleans is complex.

Pushed to the wall, the state historian took the Solomon-like position that, while the monument was physically ordinary, straight-off-the-shelf architecture, the event and views it commemorated were genuinely historical. Reviewing courts agreed. In point of fact, the monument was undeniably racial—the entire platform of the White League was racial—and at the same time it was undeniably historical. Which made the decision excruciating.

Now the city was in a bind. It could no longer keep the monument in the warehouse, but it was damned if it wanted the thing back at the foot of Canal Street for all the world to see. The elements of compromise were delicate. The state historian insisted that the historic location of the monument mattered, but perhaps not the exact site it had previously occupied. So the city found the most obscure nearby location that it could, accessible only by a one-way street which served as a backup entry to a parking garage, shielded on the batture side by a concrete floodwall. The city then added yet another plaque which reads, opaquely, that the monument honored Americans on both sides of the battle, "a conflict of the past that should teach us lessons for the future." What exactly those lessons are is left for us to say.

One answer can be found on a one-way street leading to a parking garage, hemmed in by a floodwall, close by but no longer on the river in the heart of New Orleans. It is a statue and it will not go away.

Batture at New Orleans, 1841. Courtesy of Louisiana Collections, Tulane University Libraries.

Skiff and keelboats at New Orleans. Courtesy of Louisiana Collections, Tulane University Libraries.

Loading cotton wagons. Courtesy of Louisiana Division/City Archives, New Orleans Public Library.

Steamboat with raised gangway. Courtesy of Louisiana Division/City Archives, New Orleans Public Library.

Dockworkers sleeping. Courtesy of Louisiana Division/City Archives, New Orleans Public Library.

New Orleans levee scene, from *Frank Leslie's Illustrated Newspaper*, January 8, 1881. Courtesy of Louisiana Collections, Tulane University Libraries.

Cotton Expo. Courtesy of The Historic New Orleans Collection, accession no. 1974.25.2.192.

Ames Crevasse, 1873. C. Milo Williams, photographer. C. Milo Williams Photographic Prints Collection, Southeastern Archive, Special Collections Division, Tulane University Libraries.

Audubon Park. Courtesy of The Historic New Orleans Collection, accession no. 1979.325.5761.

Picnic in the Cannes Brulees. C. Milo Williams, photographer. C. Milo Williams Photographic Prints Collection, Southeastern Archive, Special Collections Division, Tulane University Libraries.

Shack on the batture. Courtesy of The Historic New Orleans Collection, accession no. 1974.25.31.56.

Low water at Carrollton. Courtesy of Louisiana Division/ City Archives, New Orleans Public Library.

Boy on log debris. Courtesy of Louisiana Division/City Archives, New Orleans Public Library.

Boys on a raft. Courtesy of Louisiana Division/City Archives, New Orleans Public Library.

Repairing the revetment
at Carrollton. Courtesy of
Louisiana Division/City
Archives, New Orleans
Public Library.

New Southport
Club. Courtesy of
The Historic New
Orleans Collection,
accession no.
1979.325.144.

Clothes pole man. Courtesy of
Louisiana State Museum.

Carrollton Railroad Station. Courtesy of The Historic New Orleans Collection, accession no. 1975.25.37.173. C. Milo Williams, photographer.

Trepagnier plantation. Courtesy of The Historic New Orleans Collection, accession no. 1978.70.109.

FERRY

We come into the city for the first time along the river, two boys in the back seat, six years old and three, face deep in a nest of comic books, food wrappers, pillows, and a slingshot I purchased in a moment of weakness at a truck stop in Tennessee called Mad Harry's. Driving into Dixie, all the gas stations seemed to carry names indicating the mental instability of the owner. Lisa says that is to show how low his prices are. We are sodden with fatigue.

Suddenly Gabriel's voice pipes up from the back seat. "Look! Trains!" and there it is, a train as long as an anaconda, but it is not out in front of us. It is in the sky. The cars stretch from one bank of the river to the other, out of sight on both ends, crawling up and over the Huey Long bridge so slowly that you wonder if they will make it, the rust-red boxcars from my childhood with their exciting logos: Rock Island, Route of the Rockets, Southern Pacific, The Western Way. We see new tank cars, too, all black, anonymous as bombs, their chemicals stenciled in white codes so the first responders don't kill themselves. We pull over to watch. I rode the boxcars one summer and a flatcar of squared-off logs from Wenatchee, Washington, to Chicago. I am seeing my past. The boys are seeing something out of their picture books. And this is before we see the ferries.

The New Orleans ferries are magic. They cross the Mississippi River so close to water that you can feel the spray and almost touch the gulls wheeling overhead, one shore receding and a new world approaching; we are with Christopher Columbus, ready to land.

Our first drive downtown is a disappointment of traffic, roadside trash, and streets that simply disappear until we get to the batture and find a ferryboat called the *Thomas Jefferson*. We had no idea it was there. We ride over to Algiers Point and I lean against the rail, oblivious to my boys' delight and to Lisa's worry that they'll go overboard, lost in another memory.

I am crossing the Hudson River with my father. It is a special day; he is taking me to New York City, to his office, I do not remember why. We get off the train at the Port of Newark along with hundreds of similar-looking men in dark suits and gray hats who are very determined and walking fast, briefcases in one hand, newspapers in the other, down a rushing tunnel and across a plank walkway and onto one of several waiting ferries, heaving slightly in the pitch of the river, the water sloshing underneath and then, ominously, disappearing. Suddenly the engines churn, and we are on the open water. The men jam the decks, Wall Street bankers and advertising executives rubbing elbows with taxi drivers and elevator operators, the upstairs-downstairs of the working city for one brief moment equal under the sky. They take off their hats, hair to the breeze, smile, small-talk to each other. How about those Yankees! Didn't it rain yesterday! It all might end, and will indeed end, the moment they get to the far shore, but here, for this brief wink of the day, they are friends with each other and the river and the rising morning. They are transformed.

The undoing of ferries was time. I got into trouble one weekend fishing down at Point a la Hache with Charlie Bosch, who ran the Louisiana Wildlife Federation in the early 1970s. Among his other duties Charlie kept legislators supplied with enough liquor and companionship to enact the state's first environmental laws and keep them afloat. The game was wide open in those days. The fishing was wide open, too; you measured a good weekend not by the number of fish but by the number of ice coolers you filled, a two-chest day, old lunkers and juveniles, it didn't matter, life had no limits.

Only on this occasion the weather was frigid, the wind blew stiffly out of the north, and we were thoroughly skunked, not even a flounder, nothing to take home. Seeing our predicament from the dock, a friend of Charlie's, who wrote an outdoor column called "Sink the Hook Hard," gave me a Styrofoam cooler of fresh-trawled shrimp. I still lived in Washington, D.C., at the time and had a 3 p.m. flight from New Orleans. Between the camp and the airport was a ferry.

We missed it. We topped the levee at Belle Chase just in time to watch it pull away, and waited forty long minutes for its return. Charlie remained upbeat. He had driven bulldozers with the Sea-bees during World War II, and his idea of travel was pedal to the floor and straight ahead. The ride that followed was a blur of fright-ened drivers getting out of our way, angry horns and return waves of Charlie's unlit cigar, but I was at the check-in counter with eight minutes to go. I threw them my shrimp cooler and ran to the gate. I made it. Of course, the cooler did not.

Some days later I received a call from National Airport. A Sty-rofoam object had arrived with my name on it. They described the sides as "bulging," and apparently it had an odor. Would I please come and pick it up. I said that there must be some mistake, that was not my cooler, which I suppose was technically correct. It be-longed to Charlie's friend. On reflection, had there been a bridge at Belle Chase instead of a ferry across the river I would have made the flight ahead of time, saved the shrimp, eaten them, and forgotten all about it. Which is the point; on time, and minus the journey.

I read reports today that the New Orleans ferries are not mak-ing money, they are losing money, and the implications seem clear. Of course the ferries are not making money, how could they, un-less you count the other currency they provide to the city and the people who use them and the rest of us who enjoy their possibili-ties, watching them weave their little shuttles, bold as hunting dogs, timing their moves, threading their way past the tugs and ships going up and down the river on its ever-shifting current, a ballet of trajectories that are as beautiful as they are impossible to quantify. That one fact alone may be their undoing.

Imagine a state that runs long trains upriver and over the high bridge at Huey P. Long. Imagine a place with working ferries, every half hour, free for bikes and pedestrians, a couple of dollars for cars. Imagine a place with woods along the river, not a park, just trees and no rules, no admission fee. Imagine a world without them, without even the memory of them. I can still see my father on the Hudson River ferry, hatless, face to the morning sun. He is smiling.

CYCLING

SOMEONE BROKE INTO THE TOOL SHED and took our bicycles. We had four in all but mine was the oldest by far with a large yellow child's seat still mounted on the back, its anchor nuts rusted to the frame. As the boys outgrew the seat it remained handy for carrying my books back and forth to school, the kind of adaptation that Darwin described with the beaks of finches a century and a half ago. The day after the theft I walked out front and found my bicycle on the grass. Not Lisa's bike or those of the boys, only mine. It was on its side, yellow seat yawning at me like the mouth of a plastic monster. Whoever stole it, returned it.

Lisa says they returned it because they couldn't get the seat off. That makes sense, but I have always suspected another dimension. A child's seat implies the presence of a child, and I am thinking that it struck the conscience of an adult, somewhere, somehow connected to the perpetrators. The adult said, that's a *baby's* seat, you can't take a bike from a baby. Got to give it back. That is what I'd like to think, anyway.

So while other cyclists move up to spandex shorts and the multiple gears of the biking world, you will see me on this old junker with the yellow seat in back that I have ridden so many times up and down the levee and, when the day is free, to make a loop out to Lake Pontchartrain and then back by the Mississippi. Then there is the really big loop, up the river and around the lake entirely. We have only done that one once, Lisa and I, and I doubt I would to do it again. For openers, I underestimated the length of that trip by about forty miles.

Bicycle trips look easier than they turn out to be. The lines on the map are so clear. This is what I was showing my students one Saturday on a trip to the lake, sitting around the table at Sid Mar's restaurant, the gulls from Pontchartrain circling outside the porch screens. I was drawing a map on a napkin, a few clean lines, keeping it simple, because most of these kids had been living in New Orleans for less than a month and were going to go back to town on their own. A few others and I were going to ride west along the lake, circle past the airport to the river, and come home on the levee path. It is normally a good run, but this was one of those Octobers that would not let summer go and the heat was sweltering. We had already come through two thunderstorms that rather than clear the air simply turned it into a sauna. So I can't blame anyone for turning back, I said. Only half meaning it.

Eventually, they made it home, led by a colleague who was also new to town and who, misreading the map, biked them instead down to the Faubourg Marigny on the far side of the Quarter. They beat their way several extra miles uptown along the trolley line. As it worked out, they had the easier run. Ours turned into a death march as we ran out of drinking water, were slowed by flat tires, and saw our party dwindle one by one to call a friend for a pickup. By the time we got to the airport we were down to four, circling the perimeter and watching the planes come in low over the cypress trees. It seemed as if we could reach up and touch the wheels, catching the eyes of passengers who were white-knuckling it in.

By midafternoon we had reached the Mississippi River, which was the good news. The bad news was that there had been no shade since leaving Sid Mar's three hours ago, and we were cooking like boiled eggs. So we did the only reasonable thing, which was also the unthinkable thing, and jumped in the river to cool off. In late summer the river has retreated from the batture and remains shallow for many yards out. Then it drops precipitously to an unmeasurable depth and you do not want to follow. The trick is to get out far enough to get wet, rolling around in the shallows, without taking that extra step. If I were to put this activity on a law school exam concerning negligence, the verdict against me would be unanimous, but at times you find yourself in these situations. We simply had to cool off. We pretended we were hippos. But I do not recommend it.

The ride home was easier on the paved path, up in the breeze. Originally, the path was made of rangia clam shells that were dredged from reef beds in Lake Pontchartrain. The shells crushed flat to make a porous surface, easy to maintain. Dredging companies bought licenses from the state for pennies on the acre and sold the shells back to the state for a fortune. Their big suction pipes with heads six feet across worked the lake bottoms back and forth, turning the former reefs and grassbeds into a lifeless gel. Within a few decades the great fishing grounds at the back door of New Orleans, the shrimp and crab boats bringing their catch in to the Turning basin, had been decimated. Only the water remained. It took two lawsuits and an administrative hearing to shut shell dredging down.

Which nearly shut down bicycling on the levee top as well. You could ride the shell path on any bicycle in the old days, not all that rapidly, but it was fine. When the shells were replaced by crushed stone, however, bike wheels would sink in and die like those truck traps they build on the downslope of mountain roads to stop the eighteen-wheelers. Ending shell dredging was step one in restoring Lake Pontchartrain, but cyclists paid a price, until New Orleans and Jefferson caught onto the idea of paving the levee top, which they did. Biking that stretch today is an amenity that most cities of the country would kill to have at hand.

The problem is that the paved top ends at the St. John Parish line, opposite a sweeping bend at Ormond Plantation. From then on a touring bike has two options. You can turn around and go home, or you can drop down to River Road and play roulette with the passing cars. They are, in fact, mostly trucks, they are going fast, they seem to get wider every year, and there is no shoulder to that stretch of road, none. There are also a number of impatient drivers who will come up behind a bicycle and blast the horn, as if that would make you disappear. Luckily, the run to the spillway is relatively short, and so long as you don't time it when the refineries are letting out at Shell and Valero you are at no more risk than you usually are on Louisiana roads. Which is not to say, safe. You have no idea how high that risk is until you do the big loop around Lake Pontchartrain, at the end of which you will have seen it all.

Lisa and I are at a small store near Ponchatoula. We have biked upriver to LaPlace, crossed over Pass Manchac with the big red crab on the restaurant roof and, sagging by now, limped north looking for refills on water and anything with salt on it or sugar in it. "Oh you poor darlings," the store lady says to us, for the first of many times over the next two days. Not about the biking. She can't believe that people like us live in New Orleans. "My sister used to live down there," she says. "Back before you know." It is clear to her that the only white people left in New Orleans are those in for-tresses on St. Charles Avenue or without the means to move out, which apparently explains our plight. I down three chocolate milks and say thanks.

The real disbelief, however, occurs on the roads themselves, par-ticularly the highway along the north side of the lake, which carries every manner of vehicle from passenger cars to tow trucks and they all share one characteristic in common: they cannot accept that there are bicycles on the road. The more polite ones simply sound their horns and speed by, not yielding an inch. There is a small shoulder along here, but it is filled with cans and broken glass. Life is full of choices, and choosing the glass or the road is one of them. We choose road, me in the lead, which is a mistake because then Lisa is the one they come up on from behind so she takes the first blow. Mostly it is just insults out the passenger window, rapidly rolled down for better communication, but at times the whole arm sticks out as if to push her away. We quickly change order, and I am next greeted by a pickup whose driver is disadvantaged because he is alone in the vehicle and on the wrong side of it to dish out real abuse, so he swerves at us, reaches over, opens the passenger door and starts shoveling trash out in front of us while yelling, "Go ride in the fucking *park!*"

I do not react well to these situations. Once up on the Natchez Trace where the speed limit is said to be forty-five miles per hour, although if any vehicle were to drive that slowly it would be crushed from the rear, a heavy truck passed so close to us that the draft blew me off the road. When I swerved back I was yelling at his mud flaps and giving him the universal, one-finger indication of disapproval. I climbed the next hill, still fuming, to find him on the other side, parked and waiting. He was out of the cab and walking towards me, punching his fists together like an anxious boxer, and I did the only thing I could do, attack. I said, "You almost killed me back there, damn it, you almost took my life!" He looked the slightest bit confused, but I apparently slowed him down and that was all it took because over the rise behind me came Lisa at that very moment and he suddenly added one and one. At the very least she would be a witness. So he cussed me out and I maintained my mad face and somehow the wise hen saved the two male cocks from doing something stupid, and here I am to tell about it.

The beauty part of cycling the levee top is the absence of automobiles. I'll grant you that bikers can run red lights, come up one-way streets the wrong way, and weave slowly and unsteadily ahead of your windshield. It can be difficult to trust that they will stay over there while you go here. But this does not explain the violence which seems prompted not by the cyclist but by the fact that bicycles are out there at all. Lisa says that they are just people in a hurry. Me, I think it is something in the male mind. None of these people are women. I have never been put at risk by a female driver, except by some coed leaving the daiquiri shop and glued to her cell phone who never saw me in the first place. So what does that mean?

This evening I may go down to the levee for a spin. I am already looking forward to it, and it is only one in the afternoon.

PAGGIO

"WATCH OUT FOR THE JERK," says Lisa, who is watching a little more carefully than I am because I've been driving the last leg since Alabama. We are new to the city, and everything on Oak Street near the levee looks like it came from my childhood, circa 1945. There is a green shack with a rusty bicycle hanging out front like an advertisement for a saloon—wait, it may *be* a saloon—a lot full of what look like marble pillars, and a store that says Five And Dime. What is right ahead of us, however, is a sports car, stopped dead in the middle of the road. I brake and wait. The driver's door opens and an arm extends below it to the street to deposit the box of a hamburger to go. Then, in sequence, part of the roll, a wax paper drink cup, its lid, several napkins, ketchup packages, some loose fries, and a straw. The driver then cleans her hands with the remaining napkin and drops it neatly on the pile. It didn't take a minute. She was cleaning up.

I wish I could say it was an exception, but there is something in the genes here that allows people to empty the car ashtray on your curb with an absolutely clear conscience, watch their dog poop on your sidewalk while they are talking to you, and scatter their food wrappers like confetti and still enjoy the music, as if it all went away to the great repository in the sky.

On my last trip to the airport I saw a snowy egret with wings like a wedding gown rise from a canal littered with plastic bags and two shopping carts. There is no bird more beautiful, and no backdrop more ugly. You wonder what other people see. I think the answer is that they see the same thing and it looks perfectly normal.

One good thing about trash, it is an easy way to find the summer camp of Ricky and the boys. You just look for signs that they were here yesterday. As I am walking up I hear one of them say, "Watch out for that motherfucker," which gives me pause until I realize that they are not talking about me but about a light-skinned black man who is whirling a huge naked saber out on the sand. He stands tall, head shaven, bare feet, wearing only the baggy trousers of the martial arts. His shirt and sandals are stacked neatly by the water. His sword slashes the air in bursts, down and up, then a leaping turn and he cuts from behind. When he finishes he stands stock still, bows to the river, breathes deeply, and begins again. He is in his own space out here on the batture, public and private, safe and dangerous, all at the same time. Out here, this looks perfectly normal, too.

Giving the master a wide berth, I come into the shade along the river, picking my way over the most recent debris. To be fair, they have a garbage bag hung on a tree near by, but also to be fair, it would take ten bags and a Boy Scout troop to get this place in order. Which raises the question that has come to haunt me here; what is order and why is it so important?

About a year ago a fellow copied me on a letter he'd written asking the city to cut down all of these unsightly batture trees. He lived nearby, he said, and the woods harbored rats and other unattractive animals. I don't think he said that they harbored unattractive people, but he could have. I wrote him back and said that there were actually some attractive things down there; you could see the raccoons hopping the levee in late summer, humpbacked like little camels, and if you removed the trees all he'd likely see is the trash washed up by the river and a line of monster barges, rusting at anchor. But suppose, he wrote back, the parish cleaned the place up and made it a park? I said that would be a miracle, more likely they'd just post it off limits, but examining my heart I think I was fearing something different. They might *actually* clean it up and that would be the end of what it is. There would be no room left for the beavers that work the willows by the sewage and water board outfall, the roosting hawks, the deadbeats fleeing custody payments, the guy twirling his huge saber, or Ricky and the boys out for an evening with their Budweisers and the river sky. Whether you can have clean and all this, too, is a good question. But I think the answer is no.

If you want clean you can find it at the Fly, a mile downriver behind Audubon Park, and it is a splendid facility, built on a berm, the river safely removed by a sloping groin of rocks, and rimmed with a tidy sidewalk like any respectable neighborhood. There used to be a dirt hill at one end of the Fly, the joy of many kids including ours who climbed up on all fours and slid down on seat bottoms and came over from time to time with scrapes bleeding from dirty knees. It was, of course, a magnet for fun, and it has since been torn down and replaced by a play set of plastic and metal tubes, on top of something like rubber soil. It is not easy to fly a kite up there anymore either, because the grassy plain has been marked off for sports events and studded with backstops and soccer goals. If you are not in this league or another, you are trespassing. With the exception of the boats going by on the river, which is, granted, a major exception, we could be in downtown Atlanta. It is very nice here on the Fly, green, convenient, and open to the breeze, but it is not the same.

For one thing you can't net grass shrimp for bait. These are real shrimp about the size of your thumbnail, translucent as water, their innards showing like an X-ray, and they are irresistible to perch, sac-o-lait, and the next fish up the chain. They live in the shallows along the batture woods and you catch them like catching blue-shell crabs, but instead of placing the net down and baiting them to come over it, you scoop the net under their hideouts, the submerged sticks and leaves in the water, and shake them down. You need the woods.

I met a man named Paggio who lived on the batture of the Atchafalaya River, the only person I ever knew to do that. He lived simply, as in a hut with a rusty bed spring, a kerosene stove, and green anoles running up the walls. The commerce of his life began with grass shrimp. He broke off tree branches and stuck them, leaves and all, upside down at the edge of the water. A few hours later he'd come along, lift the branches and shake them out into a can, grass shrimp falling like raindrops, which he'd use for bait for small fish, which he'd use as bait for larger ones. He kept his big ones alive on a line in the water for days, waiting for one of the tugs to come down river. They'd toot their horns and call out, "HEY, PAGG-EE-OO!" and he'd raise his arms and they'd pull over to shore and he'd swap out fresh fish for something hard to drink and cans of peas. My guess is that they gave him something from the pantry anyway, fish or no.

I'm told, lest you are wondering, that Paggio bathed once a month when he motored over to the levee on the west side of the floodway and went visiting a house in New Iberia where the ladies paid attention to him for money. Not much money, I should think, because he didn't have much money. The story goes that they made him wash, very thoroughly, so you could say that it had something to do with personal hygiene, too. It all seemed to work, and keep him alive, but Paggio is gone now and no one else is likely to take his place.

Which is what I am talking about. I am not sure that you can have these things both ways.

HOMICIDE

Lisa calls out, "Be safe," as we walk out the door. We take it idly, the dog and I, but Lisa means it. There have been some shootings lately, and a neighbor mowing his lawn last weekend ran over a loaded pistol. I say, "We will," over my shoulder but what I am really thinking is that we are safer out on the batture these days than any other place in the city. I mean, a venue where nobody carries any money and most people you come across have absolutely nothing to steal. Someone is going to try to rob Ms. Bear?

It is Friday evening and a busy one down by the levee at Cooter Brown's. Several dozen trucks and pickups are spread out on the crushed limestone along the railroad tracks, a few up on the grass. Across the street from Cooter's the Daiquiri Shop is also in full swing, the commuters loading up on the hard stuff before heading out to the interstate and the drive home. The daiquiri establishment used to have a drive-in service that passed containers of rum and fruit juice the size of milk shakes through the car windows, several per vehicle, but the federal agency that hands out highway money frowned on the practice and the fun stopped. Now you actually have to get out of your car.

Ms. Bear stops to sniff at the tires and any food that might have fallen out of car doors, and I take a quick inventory. From the look of the vehicles, the testosterone index is hovering between orange and red. On one row a single passenger car is surrounded by a phalanx of Pathfinders, Trackers, Trailblazers, and other vehicles to destinations that only real men can get to like Tundra and Yukon, to say nothing of Silverado. Where, we assume, there are no other such vehicles to be found. We find a new one, Bravada, which must have turned into an accolade when I wasn't looking, and there at the end, the Armada, which has always made me pause. Does anyone remember what happened to the Armada?

I think about matching the names of these vehicles with their drivers and seeing exactly who it is these days Pathfinding the big Bravada across the Tundra to Silverado. Most likely a mom at Wal-Mart. At first blush, these are rather innocent illusions. Until one comes to the gasoline they swallow and what we do to the rest of the world in order to get it. At this point innocence gives way to real places, wasted landscapes, and fires in the night.

We mount the levee and enter our other world, heading down towards the sand flats under the power lines. I have slipped Bear's leash. She is padding around the tree line and her eyes are lit like Christmas morning, so many smells and rustles. Lisa's "be safe" has triggered a chain reaction in my mind, however, and I am going with it. There is a lot of homicide floating around New Orleans, random, casual, an ad hoc guerilla war. Five shootings on a recent weekend, and they were not an anomaly. The following Monday someone killed a minister and his wife because a relative of theirs—not them, a relative—was going to testify as a witness to yet another killing. This morning's paper, along with the usual shootings, reported the verdict in the homicide trial of a rap star with the apocalyptic name of C-Murder. The decision was apparently so difficult for the jurors that they dissolved into trauma and vomiting, despite the testimony of two eyewitnesses. One of the witnesses, granted, was a hoodlum. But you rarely have Christ's apostles to testify in a street shooting.

Many years ago, a young man then, I was prosecuting a murder case in the District of Columbia against a drug dealer with the more user-friendly street name of Rabbit. His partner was called Beaver, and the full team included such luminaries as Bootnose, Knuckles, Twitty, Blood, Fat 'n Nasty, and Big Joe Cunningham. Normally, when people messed up the dope, used it instead of selling it, Mr.

Cunningham took them out to the interstate median strip at peak traffic flow and put his fighting dogs on them. They had nowhere to run. But it seems that a dealer named Ricky messed up big time and needed to become a lesson. Rabbit took him to an abandoned house and shot him in the head.

Our problem was that we had only one witness, a stone-junkie named Clarence, who was administering a dose of heroin to himself in the downstairs bathroom when Rabbit pulled the trigger. Clarence was the key to our case, and we kept him that way by sending federal agents out on the street to purchase things to make him happy. It happens. The mindset was this: Rabbit was a killer and had to go down. We had an even more tricky problem with Clarence, though, which was that he would testify that he saw Rabbit shoot Ricky at the foot of the stairs, outside the bathroom door. At which point Ricky fell upstairs to the second floor landing. We could not shake Clarence from the gravity-defying notion that the body fell up a full flight of stairs, but in the end it did not seem to matter. The jury convicted. You take your witnesses as you find them, and hope.

The statistics in New Orleans these days are daunting. We lead the nation, each year, for homicides per capita, this last year at 67 deaths per 100,000 residents. The city, which depends on tourism for life support, has protested the number, claiming that with more residents back from Katrina the rate is only 57 per 100 grand. Unfortunately, even if this were true it would not change the ranking. The next closest murder capitol, St Louis, came in at 47, and the remaining top ten cities dropped into the 30s and 20s. Houston, we have a problem.

I am down on the sand flats now, sitting against a stump that has washed ashore. Out on the dead calm surface of the Mississippi purple martins are having an evening feast, twisting and diving over the trees to catch insects and then down to the water to nip a drink, restless as bullets in the air. They too, are killing, but as part of a life cycle that antedated humans by more millennia than we can get our minds around. The New Orleans killings are part of a kill-your-own-kind death cycle almost unknown to other species. What is it about this city? Other metropolises on the ropes have their share of poor, undereducated and underemployed people, some like Detroit and Baltimore chronically so. Yet, down here, we lead the nation in murder.

It may be in the genes, if cities have genes, and if not they certainly have histories that act like genes and the DNA of New Orleans is unmistakably homicidal. It could have begun with the first boatloads from France that, to the despair of Bienville LeMoyne, brought a high percentage of cut-purses and prostitutes, hustled off the streets of Paris in a land scheme so fraudulently mounted that it soon collapsed. A century later, the city had turned into a self-described "hell on earth" where death by violence exceeded that of any other place in America short of, perhaps, for a brief shining moment, Tombstone, Arizona, which was the size of a postage stamp. Two thirds of New Orleans homicides are said to have taken place in The Swamp and other slums, which also means, however, that one third did not. Near the onset of the Civil War, the *New York Tribune* called murder an "every day occurrence" in New Orleans, and a local paper complained that "the record of one deed of blood hardly dried upon the paper" before it was followed by another. The culture of killing, however, went deeper. It was also a regional pastime.

It started with the Creoles, but soon anyone who was anyone was challenging a rival to a duel. The city saw hundreds of white-collar shootings a year, as many as a dozen under the oaks in City Park on any given Sunday, with doctors, lawyers, newspaper editors, and politicians up to Governor Claiborne readying their seconds, marking out their paces, and turning to engage in the maiming or execution of someone who had offended their honor. Until the Civil War, it was said that there was "rarely a man in public office who had not fought one duel, in most cases several." They used pistols, of course, but broadswords, epees, knives, shotguns, and even cypress rails from nearby fences would do as well. What mattered was not the weapon, but the notion of honor and the thrill of death. I am wondering what has changed. Perhaps it remains, today, all about honor and the thrill of death. Only, different people are claiming it.

Shootings, today, are on the front page of the daily paper, dominate the metro section, and lead the television evening news. With political activity limited to election cycles and football material thin for half the year, they seem to be a form of daily entertainment, as macabre as the Roman spectaculars. You get the funnies, the murders, and the sports. I have come to teach overseas in the summers, and the first thing that strikes Lisa and me is the scarcity of news about criminal activity of any kind, and no celebration of homicide. I'm sure that they happen, but they are not a centerpiece of life. Maybe Americans are evolving into a different species, one that is both trapped in and fascinated by its own violence. I recall reading of the members of a Greek society who celebrated their notion that life was meaningless by jumping out of the window to their deaths. More or less proved their point, I suppose.

Ms. Bear comes up next to me and begins licking my hand. It is not so much about affection; she is hungry and this is not where her food bowl lives. She brings me back into the present where the purple martins are gone and the river is backlit with lights from the power plant across the way. We're going to be late getting back. Lisa will think we are not being safe, and she is probably right. But I am glad I was by the water for a while and able to think about this killing business which at some level rubs against everyone who lives here. Today's wilderness is not to be conquered by Pathfinders on their way to Silverado or, for that matter, to the far suburbs. It is right here.

EVEN

Before I get within sight of the clearing I can hear a voice say, "It's a *dog*," as if it might have been a wolf or a tiger, and then it says, "Look out! It's going for your leg," and then I appear. They stop talking, connecting me to Ms. Bear who had gone in first. I say, "She's fine, not a bite in her." They just sit there, three black boys in stone, looking at the white man who had come onto their scene.

This is the clearing that Ricky and others occupy for most of the year, but they move out in summer to the shade of a few trees under the power lines, down by the water where they can catch the breeze from the south and swim their dogs. I passed them today coming in, and I could tell Ricky was with them from a distance because I could see his bike. If bicycles were tanks, his would be the General Pershing model, with its rusty fenders, rearview mirror, light, bell and a squeegee horn duct-taped to the handlebar, two enormous baskets in the rear, and a coffee can wired to the steering post where he carries whatever beverage he is working on at the time. I have seen him come over the levee hauling boxes of canned goods and pieces of rug, anything that might make the woods more comfortable, and leaving in the evening carrying odd bits of driftwood that he will sand, stain, varnish, inlay with cut glass, and turn into icons for St. Agnes Church, which is apparently his second base of operations. Today, out where they were gathered, I could see a lounge chair on the riverbank—where in the world did *that* come from?—and they had a radio tuned to the LSU game in Baton Rouge.

Leaving them for the woods, it feels as moist as the tropical bird exhibit at Audubon Zoo, the wraparound silence, and it is here that I give Ms. Bear her head and am content to follow. Only, the dog has come upon the boys in the clearing, and, just as they said, she has headed straight for a log. Maybe someone had eaten something and left the wrappers behind. Soon her head disappears and she is industriously burrowing underneath. It must be something good, I think, and right then the tallest of the three boys looks up and says to me, "Give me a dollar?"

It shouldn't have struck me the way it did, but it did. I should have just called Ms. Bear and moved on, but I didn't. It was phrased as a question but it sounded like something else and, heat rising, I say, "What is it about me . . . I'm white so I give you a dollar? What makes it ok to ask me for a dollar?" At which point I catch myself and collect the dog and walk away, but not without saying "Jesus!" as if only He could save a world so lacking in whatever I feel it lacked. Within seconds the trees have swallowed me up and I feel my anger disappear as if I were waking from a dream. As if it had never happened.

Bear soon disappears, too, and when I see her next she has tracked her way to a fishing spot on the bank which is usually strewn with old bait, Grade A habitat for dogs, or my dog anyway. The sad fact is that this dog will eat just about anything, and if it has passed through another animal first all the better. If Lisa or I are walking her through the neighborhood we keep her on a close leash. But she has developed countermeasures. She will scent the next dog dropping long before we see it and trot right on past in a dignified manner, winning herself some slack in the line, only to spring back suddenly and snatch a bite before we can yank her away. I tell Lisa that it is all part of the game, but she has more practical concerns, like the dog then licking us or throwing up undigestibles. I have to admit both do happen.

Out in the batture, however, it is a different story because the whole point of going there is to explore. This is a windfall for the dog because she not only gets to eat forbidden things but gets to roll in them as well. My part of the bargain is that I wash her afterwards. One afternoon out by Lake Maurepas while I was strapping a canoe to the roof of the car, Ms. Bear found a dead deer in the bushes. I didn't realize what had happened until she hopped into the back seat covered with slick and smelling like rancid whale. We drove the car with the windows open for days. Mostly, however, I can wash it off.

About an hour later the dog and I are returning from the woods below, and I can hear the same boys in the clearing ahead. Feeling a little ashamed of myself at this point, I am determined to just say hello and pass through, but Ms. Bear has other ideas. The conversation ends abruptly as we come onto the big fire ring with raised logs and a winter's worth of Ricky's and the boys' cans around it like a rest stop specializing in beer. The boys are on one log, looking down, not saying a thing, and the dog has gone back under the same log next to them to forage. She has probably been thinking about this log from the time we left it, and wastes no time submerging. "Bear!" I call to her, but it is useless, because when it is me against food there is no contest, and I don't even repeat the gesture.

Now she is peddling backwards, pulling something out with her jaws, and I am reminded that, although we have no idea what breeds went into this dog, the veterinarian says that part of her was a "ratter" that pulled small beasts from their holes. Four pairs of eyes are now on the dog and her prey, which becomes visible from one end, and then elongates as it meets the light of day. It is about eighteen inches long and about three inches around, dark in color, the biggest human turd I have seen. She is tugging it gently, reverently, as if knowing that to pull too hard risks breakage.

Before I can react, the tallest boy says to no one in particular and to all of us at once, "Man, that dog eats *shee-it!*" It was not a hostile comment. Rather, it was said in wonder, as if remarking on a new discovery. This is what white guys let their dogs do. Could be why they take 'em to the woods. But hanging there in the air, the comment soon turns bold, and all three of them are looking at me like a strange form of human being, one whose dog eats human turds, which is also about how I am feeling.

I have to nudge Ms. Bear away from her treasure with the point of my toe, and unable to think of anything to say I leave the clearing to the boys. I can hear excited whispers of their conversation behind us, but I do not stop to listen. I had my moment, and they have had theirs. We are even.

GYPSUM

On a summer day so still the only oxygen in New Orleans was down by the river and the woods on the batture held the heat like a furnace, out of the trees staggered a tall man wearing black boots, black jeans, an unbuttoned black vest, black hat, and an assortment of neck chains, and dragging an enormous wooden cross. From a distance he looked like Jesus in a cowboy movie. It was Ricky, instead, and it took him several minutes to haul the cross to the riverbank, lay it down, and start taking off his clothes. Stripped to only his undershorts, he waded into the water and sat down. I could hear him saying, "Ahhhh!"

As I approached, Ricky submerged completely and then came up like a hippo, blowing air and grinning. His face was covered with a coating of silt. The mud in his hair made a kind of gray plaster on dark locks. He looked supremely happy; he was mud man. The very next day, by chance, I saw the same look in a newspaper photo of a boy in a river on the other side of the world. The boy's head was coated with a gray clay that all but shut his eyes. Out of the clay he was smiling. He didn't have a clue.

The news story started here with a corporation named Freeport McMoRan, the city's only member of the Fortune 500. Freeport owned several fertilizer plants upstream that brought in gypsum rock from Florida, crushed it, poured acid through it, and bled out phosphorous, for fertilizer. The piles of crushed waste, however, were several times the size of the original rock and had been rising in ever more unwieldy piles along the riverbank, taller than any natural features in south Louisiana. Freeport feared that, with heavy rains, their waste piles could fall over. It had a better idea: bleed the piles directly into the Mississippi. The difficulty was, some of the contents were nasty. Some were radioactive.

In the mid-1980s the federal government was backing away from environmental protection across the board, and Freeport received its discharge permit without a blink. There was a small hitch, however. Louisiana would have to permit the discharge too. Normally, this was no hitch at all because Louisiana, as many southern states, took the view that environmental requirements were an obstacle. Its job was to shepherd industry past them. The state environmental agency referred to industry as its "clients" and to the public as "others," which gave you a pretty good idea of where you stood.

The one agency unhappy with all of this was the New Orleans Sewage and Water Board, which had to deliver clean water from a river carrying pollutants from a hundred industries upstream. It did not see the additional loadings from the gypsum stacks, a whopping twelve million tons a year, as good news. The board began a little crusade up the river, rounding up allies to oppose the Louisiana permit. This was not a difficult sell. These parishes, like New Orleans, depended on the river for drinking water, and nineteen of their intake pipes were within a few miles of the piles. Unlike New Orleans, they did not have sophisticated monitoring or treatment systems. These were poor, rural parishes, and they were right in front of the train.

The public hearings heated up. I entered one at city hall in New Orleans as a woman at the microphone was putting a small girl up on the lectern and saying, "I do not want her to glow in the dark!" Behind her a class from Lusher Elementary held small, handmade signs saying "Dump Jim Bob!" A short while later, *National Geographic* carried a photo of the gypsum stacks with a quotation saying that drinking water out of the Mississippi below them would be like wrapping your child's lips around the tailpipe of a car. That was me speaking, a bit over the top. The rhetoric had left the barn.

The legal problem was that the Mississippi was a big river, and tracing a particular discharge to a particular harm was all but impossible. Freeport was betting on that difficulty. During the hearing process, however, an obscure requirement surfaced that no discharge could upset the existing ratio between two elements, phosphorous and nitrogen, that produced algae blooms. Lo and behold, these waste discharges would blow the phosphorous-nitrogen ratio away.

Facing strong local opposition, the state found itself in the rare political position to actually deny a permit, and it did. It had never happened before. It has never happened since. Had it not happened here, the possibility of cleaning up the lower Mississippi would be another light year away.

Jim Bob Moffet, Freeport's chief executive, could not believe the bad press he had taken on the permit. A former local football star, he was not used to losing anything. He set out to remedy it at once, and in a time-honored way. He purchased his critics, and he paid off as many of the rest as he could. Two television journalists had reported regularly on the gypsum controversy. Both joined the company. They had been critical of Freeport; they were now on the team. He endowed separate university chairs at Tulane, Loyola, and UNO, beefed up his contributions to charities, and provided ten million dollars to start an endangered species survival center on the west bank of the river. At the opening of the center a few years later, with the state governor and city mayor in tow, he said that Louisiana businesses should "kick their [critics'] butts and send them back home." He was riding high again. Then the second shoe dropped.

Seeking new enterprises, Freeport found gold in Indonesia. "This is not a job for us," Moffett told the press, "it is a religion." Doing nothing by halves, he opened the world's largest gold and copper mine in Iryan Jaya, an island province with a thriving indigenous population and no love for the national government. It was a risky place to invest; Freeport received insurance from the U.S. government and guards from the Indonesian military. There were tales of government abuse, serious ones, as in forced labor, beatings, rape, and even murder. As the tales surfaced, western reporters tried to access the scene to verify them but found themselves blocked. If you wanted in, you went on the company's terms. The *Times-Picayune*, walking on eggs, assigned the story to its business reporter.

Human rights claims stemming from Freeport's mine played out for years, eventually dismissed by local courts as being the wrong place to try them. What emerged in the process, however, was what the mine had done to the river below and its people. On the one hand, it was providing schools and jobs. But wastes from the Grasberg mine destroyed the river for miles. The photos spoke a million words. That part was a disaster.

What followed locally was another Freeport protest. Angered by reports of human rights and environmental abuses, some of them from the Catholic Church in Indonesia, Loyola students staged a candlelight march down St. Charles Avenue to the home of Jim Bob Moffet, remaining to stand in vigil. The president of Loyola, new to the job, condemned his students' actions the following day. The president of UNO followed with a long letter to the paper; he had seen the mine, he said, and everything was fine. At about the same time, and making no mention of the Freeport mine, Tulane, Loyola, and UNO joined a full-page advertisement on behalf of Freeport in the *Times-Picayune*. Entitled "Leading By Example," the institutions expressed their gratitude towards the corporation as a "caring, corporate citizen." Other recipients of Freeport largesse rushed to the pulpit as well, including members of the congressional delegation. This was the Louisiana we all knew, back again. You pay, we'll sing.

Nothing more happened. The controversy died back. The Grasberg mine laid a huge golden egg for Freeport McMoRan. Jim Bob Moffet, however, tiring perhaps of a society that would take his money but never admit him to the Krewe of Comus, pulled his headquarters out of New Orleans and moved it to Arizona. Back in Iryan Jaya his mine wastes still go into the Ajkwa River, much of the delta has died, and there is no going back.

To the Angumne people who live there, the creation story begins with a mother and four children who lived on the Ajkwa delta. When drought came, however, and the children were dying, the mother asked them to kill her and distribute her body parts, head to the north, feet towards the sea. They did so, with heavy hearts. In the morning they awoke to find a tall mountain where they had placed their mother's head. From the mountain came a clear, running river, feeding a great garden all around.

One day in the 1980s, a photographer took a picture of a boy bathing in the Ajkwa River. His head was caked with chalky mud and, in the way of children, he was smiling. He had no clue.

FIGHT

BICYCLING UP THE RIVER ONE SUMMER MORNING, a year after Katrina, I rounded the bend by the old village of Kennertown and plunged into a painting drawn a century ago, or maybe two centuries ago. American history condenses in the mind. The women were dressed in bright, calico gowns that stretched from high collars around their necks to the tops of their thick-soled shoes. The men wore Sunday outfits of dark cloth with long tails and white shirts puffed out the front. A few had shed their coats and were holding onto their suspenders like the poles on a moving bus, talking to each other, but not to the women, who were on the banquette grass, opening wicker picnic baskets and sorting out the food. The children, and there were many of them, were miniature copies of their elders, the same dresses and formal coats, the same decorous manners. None of them were rolling on the grass. None were even sitting on it.

I stopped my bike and walked in. It seemed discourteous to blow by them. I asked where they were from, and I think they said Ohio. They were Mennonites. They had come down for a month or so to help rebuild. I talked with them for a few minutes about the Ninth Ward, where they were volunteering, and then I saw the statue behind them.

I had passed this monument many times, but it was the first time I'd really looked at it. Down at the base of the levee, towards the road, two life-sized and nearly naked men in black iron were doubling their fists and preparing to assault each other. This was not a Mennonite thing to do. And yet, here on this one spot that these gentle and committed people had chosen to picnic, back in 1870, shortly after the Civil War had come to its bloody end, on a hot May morning with crowds streaming up from New Orleans, down from Baton Rouge and places still farther away, tiny Kennertown hosted the first heavyweight championship prize fight in America. It was a thriller.

Kennertown was an unlikely location for the first of anything, much less the boxing championship of America. This was the Cannes Brulees, where the rosacane grew so thick along the batture that natives burned it to drive out cougars and bears. William Kenner came up from New Orleans in the early 1800s to settle here, married a fourteen-year-old, and gave her seven children before she died. When his business partner absconded with the business fortunes, William died, too, leaving a string of riverside plantations behind. Over time, Kennertown's major asset became the New Orleans railroad, and that's how they all got here, the two heavyweight boxers, the several dozen promoters, the newspapermen, artists and journalists, bankers and lawyers, mule skinners, pickpockets, theater managers, saloon keepers, Union army generals and Confederate army privates, gathering two hours before dawn at the Jackson Street Railroad Station to jostle their way onto the waiting cars and ride upriver to the biggest fighting event in American history, a bare-fisted ten-rounder between two Englishmen, one of them an adopted American. Pride and money were on the line. The purse was two thousand, five hundred dollars, doubled by official side bets, no record of the unofficial ones. I think of Mohammed Ali versus Sonny Liston, in Africa.

Jem Mace, at age forty, had achieved God-like status in English sport for his fighting trim, athleticism, and debonair grace. Schooled in the "boxing sciences," he had only lost two fights in his life, both to opponents he later destroyed, and had owned the English championship since 1861. Tom Allen, described as "strong as a Bashan Bull," was taller and heavier and had also been an English champion before coming to America to put on performances of "living statuary," a popular entertainment of the time. With the body of a "Hercules" he was a physique to behold. The smart money was on Mace, however, one hundred dollars to seventy. Even those odds found few takers.

It is a little sobering to appreciate what "heavyweight" meant back then. Jem Mace was five foot six inches tall and weighed 165 pounds. Tom Allen, at five foot nine, went all of 170. Men smaller than this carried their blanket rolls and forty pounds of equipment on their backs, rifles few of us now could even lift, and on a breakfast of bread and coffee walked thirty miles in a day to places like Manassas and Gettysburg, arriving in time to form up and fight before sundown.

New Orleans missed out on the championship. The city was undergoing one of its sporadic fits of clean government, and, as one writer suggested, the "sudden eruption into our city of a population of men in which the animal predominates over the intellectual" would not be without consequence. One could distinguish the undesirables, he advised, by their "broad shoulders, sweeping mustaches and flashy watch-chains," as well as their "revolvers and bowie knives." And so it was that in the predawn hours of that morning a seventy-man squadron of New Orleans police mustered at the Jackson Street station to handle the worst elements of society and funnel them firmly out of town.

Instead came, by all report, one of the most pacific championship fights in history. If there were a Mennonite version of pugilism, the 1870 championship may well qualify. As the crowd disgorged from the train just upriver from the Kennertown wharf, steps beyond the boundary of New Orleans, officials were busy inspecting and marking out the field of a neighboring sugar mill. A brisk local commerce sprang up in chairs for the spectators to sit on (rocking and cane chairs went first; within the hour they were paying top dollar for orange crates), and then a steady stream of victuals and liquor. Dice tables appeared, and others for three-card monte. Meanwhile, the ring was cornered and roped, two seats placed inside for the unheard-of luxury of resting between rounds, and by 8:30 in the morning the sun was burning off a thick mist from the river and lighting up the venue.

At a few minutes before 9:00, Tom Allen came into the ring, followed briskly by Mace and a thunderous cheering. The men were soon stripped to shorts and boots, no gloves, shirts, helmets, or mouth guards; this was boxing in the raw. Just before the fight began, Mace came over to Allen and offered a five-hundred-dollar side bet, offer refused. The stage was set for a huge upset, the American bringing home the flag.

The fight went all ten rounds. One would have to have participated in a ring sport to know just how long a round is, but from my meager experience the oxygen runs out in fifteen seconds and from then on every minute is a lifetime. Back in Kennertown it was already hot and the sun was still rising. Mace and Allen were pummeling each other with bare fists. They threw each other to the ground like grizzlies. At one point, with one of them in trouble, the other laid off to give him wind. The course of the combat, however, was clear. Allen was getting killed. By the end of the sixth round his face was pulped, both eyes swollen, and the bet against him had gone to one hundred to sixteen. Even here, few takers. In the tenth and last round a bloody Allen, still wading in, landed a hard right to Mace and was heard to quip to his opponent, "Hard work, Jem!" but he was done. The fight ended, Mace went to Allen's corner and said, "Tom, you are a game man and I wish you well."

And so in the year 1870 off the batture of an obscure little river town in Louisiana, before a rough crowd of men in the Cannes Brulees, a celebrated and hard-fought boxing championship was conducted with the dignity one would like to see in the halls of Congress or a court of law. Nothing resembling it remains, not the railroad line, nor the farms, nor the sport of boxing, which has lost its sheen and gone indoors. Kenner, meanwhile, has moved inland to the interstate and a disheartening collection of strip malls, anchored by an airport that provides a constant roar overhead and whose taxis whisk passengers in and out of the city of New Orleans along chainlink fences, drainage pits, and the backs of warehouses. That is what they see of Kenner.

Maybe it is all for the better. What passes for progress has moved away and the batture remains, green all year round, the river running by, small houses and fields along the side, and on any particular Sunday a group you would never imagine might come to enjoy it wearing calico gowns. Just below the Kennertown landing is a statue commemorating the first world heavyweight prize fight on American soil. Day in and day out, Jem Mace the English champion and Tom Allen his challenger are still slugging each other, leg muscles bulging, magnificent in black iron. If you close your eyes you can hear the crowd.

GUSTAV

On August 30, 2008, the three-year anniversary of Hurricane Katrina, we found ourselves driving out River Road, batture trees to the left, shuttered houses to the right, fleeing another storm. I had made the stay-or-go decision on the last one, and we stayed. Lisa got to call this one and so we started up the car. Besides, staying didn't seem all that interesting this time. National Guard troops were already on the streets, and the city was going into lockdown. You were outside and not on your own property, you went to jail.

Just two days earlier the mayor of New Orleans had presided over a ceremony to celebrate the city's recovery. That same week the mayor's personal photographer had organized yet another celebration of the mayor himself, also advertised as a recovery event until the *Times-Picayune* disclosed that, instead, it was all about the mayor, who then explained that the award, by honoring him, honored the city as well. Some would not have agreed. Following Katrina, the mayor so disappeared from public view that a local columnist reported him AWOL and put out a call for his whereabouts.

Here was the mayor now, though, on the recovery podium and scaling a symbolic wreath over the small crowd. New Orleans was back, he said. The crowd was small because, with uncanny timing, on that same day, almost to the hour, Katrina was coming again and most people were home packing if they were not already at the airport or on the road. The mayor himself left early to attend a briefing on the coming storm. It was called Gustav this time. After the briefing, the mayor announced that it was the storm of the century, the Mother of All Storms.

In fact, at that point Gustav was still a small swirl in the Caribbean nearly a thousand miles from New Orleans. Once it entered the Gulf, if it did not smash itself against the mountains of Cuba and disappear, its possible landings fanned out over a five-hundred-mile "cone of concern" from Florida to the Rio Grande. Nobody right on up to the White House was taking any chances on storm warnings this time, however. The best guess of the weather bureau put landfall about fifty miles west of the city. Once the storm cleared Cuba, troops, food, trailers, pumps, buses, doctors, and emergency shelters were pouring into south Louisiana. Every coastal parish in the state declared a mandatory evacuation, putting several million people on the road. Notwithstanding, the director of the Terrebonne emergency agency went off to the LSU football game.

Driving out the levee road we listened to the mayor of New Orleans on the radio. He said that he wanted to talk to the looters. He said that that special arrangements had been made for them to go directly to Angola Prison, which enjoys a near holocaust-like reputation in Louisiana. Few people leave Angola, not even feet first. It has its own cemetery by the river. Looters caught during Gustav would be put directly into Angola's "general population," the mayor said, adding, "and if that happens then may God have mercy on you." If the mayor can do anything, he can find a phrase. Some would say that is his best move.

As mothers of storms go, Gustav won no awards. The hurricane deflated as it reached the coast, veered west, brought more small damage than permanent harm, and left a lot of weary people struggling to get back home. A friend of mine who works for the Corps stayed in New Orleans, enjoyed a passing shower, and then slept outside for the next few nights while the city was quiet and the stars ran across the entire sky. Lisa and I were up in Mississippi, where we had also gone after Katrina, only to be caught by a tailing rain that pounded the area for three solid days, brought up a nearby creek, and flooded our car.

Our welcome in Mississippi is always kind. Following Katrina a former student with whom we stayed, upon learning that we had left our cat behind, drove down to New Orleans with a bogus police pass to recover it. So it was again this time in a different town, up there in the rain, power lines down, refrigerator out, no lights, the neighbors dropping by to make sure we had fresh milk and did we need flashlight batteries. Infinitely kind.

They were also wary, however. New Orleans is not their kind of place, and for that reason we might not be their kind of people. They had heard news reports during Katrina of blacks going wild in the city, and it confirmed everything they had known for two hundred years. The next they heard that refugees were being bussed north to Baton Rouge. The following morning our host awakened us with a burst of automatic rifle fire on the front lawn, out towards the woods, the turf jumping like firecrackers. As I came up he handed me the rifle and said, "Ollie, I want you to have this today." I made no move to take it. "They might be coming up the driveway," he explained, "and none of them are personal friends of mine." I have always known that New Orleans is an island, and it is becoming more of one as the land sinks around it. But it is another kind of island as well.

We talk about hurricanes, driving home. For some Louisianans the Gustav evacuation was their fourth in three years. Preparations for the next exodus are becoming as much a part of the routine as summer vacations and Christmas with the folks. We have the insurance policy, some bank records, and the photograph albums in boxes and ready to ride. Like the Tunica, the Houma, and the Chitimacha who lived here for a millennium before we came along, we are moving in and out with high water again, creatures of the storm.

We enter New Orleans along the Mississippi River, the same way we went out. Overhead the sky is blustery; big winds have been pushing in from the south for almost a week. I nearly crash the car. An enormous silhouette had just passed across the windshield, motionless in the air, jagged as the Headless Horseman and equally dark. Driving with me can be dangerous when there is a new bird around. To Lisa's relief I pull over on the shoulder and we walk up the levee, river ahead of us fringed by the batture trees.

Directly above us, fronting the wind, so close by that it feels we could touch them, is a pair of magnificent frigate birds, one of the largest flying creatures in the world. I have never found them this far inland. I have seen them once or twice when I was down fishing on the coast, after a gulf storm, blown in by the wind, taking the weather as it came, gliding shorewards with it and sure to glide back out, today, tomorrow, whenever the weather turned. They are thin birds with wingspans the size of a cape, all black except for the red throat of the male, which is round as a ball, and the white heads of the young. They are not tied to pieces of land. They are survivors.

DEWBERRIES

" . . . AND WHEN I SAW THEM COMING TOWARDS ME I threw the knife into the bushes and said, 'Officer, I'm *hurt* . . . take me to the *hospital!*'"

Ricky is in a chair on top of the levee across from Cooter Brown's, and he is talking to a round-faced, Mexican-looking fellow in another chair about a foot away, their backs to civilization, looking out through the trees at the river rolling by. It is about eight in the morning and they are both holding paper bags from the top of which peek beer cans easily a foot high. I cannot tell whether they've been to bed yet or just got up early. I couldn't guess where they slept either, not on the batture anyway, because the water is over the riverbank and into the woods below, pushing ahead of it a formidable line of debris towards the bottom of the levee. When the beer cans are empty they will join the debris like old friends.

The Mexican guy says, "That's right, Ricky," and then he says it again carefully as if practicing the language. Ricky says, "Damn *right* that's right" and pulls his beer can clear out of the bag to take a pull. It is impossible not to like Ricky because he has no front teeth, at least on the top anyways, so when he grins he shows all lips and gums like the smile of a child. It makes up for the scar on his forehead.

I ask Ricky where the chairs come from and he says, "Nice, aren't they?" They are nice, they have round seats, so I say, "Kind of like the ones at Cooter Brown," and he says, "Want one?" and he points down towards the gate that leads onto a little industrial landing and sure enough there is another chair down there. It is missing a leg.

I beg off. I'm not hung up about the chair leg, but I am out on a mission for dewberry bushes because this is the weekend they are turning big and purple, and my secret picking spot is on that very landing, out of view to the side. You have to wiggle around the fence and climb over some pipes, and there the bushes rise up like fountains, full of thorns and fruit. I've filled buckets in there. The big run comes in April, and I take them home and cook them down for jam. They taste a little different because I only put in a fraction of the sugar called for by the recipe on the box, which also warns "Do Not Alter The Proportions Of This Recipe." But if you ever measure out the amount of sugar they call for, all in one bowl, you just can't pour it in. Your teeth start aching.

The other fruit coming on this time of year is Japanese plums from the loquat trees, and I recruit a neighbor's boy to help me pick them because they are high in the air. I reach up and cut a bunch with a limb-lopper while my assistant scrambles to catch them with a fishing net on their way down. Depending on his age and skill we may leave a few smashed on the road. Sometimes a driver will slow down, lower the window, and ask what we are doing. I give out one to taste, and once in a while I'm told, you know, my grandmother used to do that. An old picture from a photograph album winks back to life, and then goes out. No sane person makes jam anymore.

I cannot tell you why, but I do. If I multiplied the time it took me by the minimum wage we would come out to about sixty dollars a pint. I got the idea of canning from a friend of Ricky's down on the batture. I ran across him eating some mulberries and he said, "Try one." I said they tasted flat. So he said, "Then you ought to try the dewberries," adding in what was for him a monster sentence, "Guy from the hardware store cans 'em." So I tried them. They were delicious.

On a day in early April, then, here I would be with a bucket of loquat at the kitchen table and the radio on because pitting these babies is going to take a while. With bad luck I run into the business news, the Dow did this or that as if it didn't always do this or that, and then perhaps an interview by Terry Gross. I am hoping that Terry will not be talking with yet another rock musician, I mean, what is to ask a rock musician? I will not reveal more about the canning process that follows except that it is messy and it chases Lisa from the house. She thinks I am going to poison someone.

This year is different, though, because the loquat are late and the dewberries are under water. Spring melt has been slow up in the northern states, and now it all comes ripping down the Missouri, Platte, Ohio, Red, White, Cache, and a dozen other rivers, and it is look out New Orleans, because it can rise several yards in no time and there are suddenly two million cubic feet per second going by, more than half the water of America, right out there where you can point your toes and sit on the chairs from Cooter Brown's. Through the chainlink fence I can see the arcs of my berry bushes rising like arms of barbed wire. From this distance they look to have ripe berries. So this is D-Day.

I tell Ricky in my best cop show voice that I'm "going in" and he gives me a big smile like this is his lucky morning because it will add to the show. I say, "Watch my dog for me," and he says, "Come here, Bear," because they know each other. Walking away I see him offering her a drink from his can.

I wade through the floating bottles, Styrofoam, and a broken life jacket of the cheap kind they use on the barges for the men who hop from one to another to rope them together and every once in a while a fellow falls in and gets crushed and nobody sees him again. The water is quick to my knees, and then to my crotch, but I know there is higher land on the industrial site so I feel my way towards the gate, and sure enough the ground seems to be rising again. Just then I hear Ricky call out, "Here Bear!" quite uselessly, because Bear is a stray dog I picked up about twelve years ago and she has a phobia about getting left behind anywhere, even by twenty feet or so.

I look back and she is struggling towards me, her nose and eyes out of the water like a small alligator. I wade back in and pull her up over my shoulder. I notice that the water smells like diesel fuel and that she had found a fish to roll in. I am already committed though, and, besides Ricky and the Mexican guy are watching, so I carry the dog around the gate and onto the site but it is not pretty in here. Water is covering the lower berries, the upper ones are sagging only inches above it, and even if they might be worth picking I'd have to clean them, and ripe dewberries don't wash off very well. They just disintegrate and go down the drain. I tell Ms. Bear it's a no-go.

When I come out, Ricky and his friend have popped new beers. The cans must have been under their shirts. The ones they emptied are nowhere in sight.

IT

"HONEY, THEY GOING TO DO WHAT?" Teresa Róbert looks out over the field between her kitchen and the Mississippi River to the green swell of the levee and, behind, the tops of the batture trees. Her friend Ruby has called. "Don't you read the paper, dawlin'?" she says to Teresa, who has two tiny boys running underfoot and another baby on the way. "Ruby," says Teresa, "I haven't got *time* to read the paper," or watch the news on television either, she is thinking. Teresa is fully occupied with the kids and running a little restaurant called The Cabin with her husband, Al. The rest of life is for other people.

"Teresa," Ruby says, "they going to build a big toxic waste plant by you, barges coming in off the river and all." She pauses, skimming the item, and then adds, "It's going to be the biggest one in the world." Teresa looks away from the tree line and begins to pace the kitchen, dangling the phone cord behind. Over the next few years her shoe heels will hammer the surface of the kitchen floor into hundreds of tiny circles as she works the telephone. Teresa Róbert now has a third job.

You can travel from New Orleans to Baton Rouge on the interstate and never see a thing, or you can take the River Road that winds along the batture as if it were driving under the influence, following the horseshoe bends, one hand out to the levee to steady yourself and on the other side a forgotten landscape of small towns, refineries, and chemical plants that light up the night sky. About an hour into the journey you come into Burnside, a row of stores, a handful of cottages, and, out across the field, an old slave quarters now restored and operated as The Cabin by the Róberts, who will end up changing everything about environmental protection in Louisiana.

Not by design. The Róberts were not revolutionaries. Al owned a fuel distributorship tied to the nearby Texaco refinery. Teresa, in her twenties, was raising children and making menus. But here was Governor Edwards announcing to the Baton Rouge *Morning Advocate* that the Industrial Tank Corporation (the name would change to International Technology as the game went on, but it was always called "IT") of California was going to build the "world's largest hazardous waste disposal facility" (a claim later reduced to the largest in the United States), on 1,100 acres of land, in Burnside. With its own loading dock and road up from the river to the treatment building, it would even look like a plantation.

Louisiana industry produces a staggering amount of hazardous waste. In the 1970s much of it was sitting around in rusting drums, or open pits, or was simply dumped into the river. One year earlier a young man named Curly Jackson opened up the cock valve of a truck full of hydrogen sulfide in a field near Bayou Sorrell and was killed on the spot by the fumes. A subsequent report by the television program *20/20* showed a reenactment of the incident, followed by an interview with Governor Edwards, who quipped, characteristically, that "you can't make an omelet without breaking eggs." The omelet he had in mind was the hazardous waste business, which was beginning to boom elsewhere in the country. He saw no reason for his home state to miss out.

What followed was a Louisiana Hayride. For openers, the state would need a hazardous waste plan. By coincidence, a Louisiana official ran into an IT representative at a meeting in California, and a marriage quickly followed. IT would do a study for the Louisiana plan. It would hire as its consultant the firm that had also been hired by the state to write the plan itself, closing the loop. Lo and behold, the plan recommended a large facility at a single site, Burnside, Louisiana, where, of all coincidences, IT had been negotiating a $1.4 million deal for the land. Within a few days after the plan's approval IT bought the site. In effect, IT had approved its own project. The governor's prediction was looking very good. There was only a state environmental review to go.

It didn't look good to the Róberts and their friend Ruby Cointment, however, who had begun to dig in. The more they dug, the worse it appeared. The IT project called for "land farming," which sounded disarmingly agricultural but turned out to consist of spreading toxic waste onto open fields and then ditching the residues into the soil. As the Róberts and others began asking questions like "What happens when it rains?" the proposal began to bounce from one treatment process to another. The company seemed to be making things up as it went along. Teresa and Ruby formed a group called Save Our Selves ("because we knew if we didn't help ourselves, nobody else would") and began collecting signatures, more than ten thousand at one point, against the plant. They funded their effort with raffles on old television sets and selling snowball cones at the Jambalaya Festival. Not without pushback. Some people who had signed the petition called Teresa to remove their names, explaining that they were told they would lose their jobs. Local chemical plants instructed their employees not to eat at the Róberts' restaurant. At one point IT approached Teresa and offered to buy three hundred lunches at The Cabin a week for its workers if she'd declare peace. Instead, she and Al took a trip.

Facing local opposition, IT offered to fly Louisiana officials to see its operations in California. Save Our Selves went along, but was careful to pay its own way. The official delegation received a brisk and upbeat tour. The Róberts, following in a rented car, saw something more like "a big joke," a waste incinerator no larger than "the one behind the food store," several buildings "spray-painted to look like aluminum," and acres of fields on which nothing grew. One part of the site was posted off limits, but before they were chased away Al and Teresa saw ponds overflowing with liquids. The stench was "unbearable." Interviews with surrounding neighbors were no more encouraging. The plant was a "nightmare," they said; it had picked up several million dollars in fines; you didn't want it in your backyard. IT's backyard in California was a community of Mexican workers. In Burnside it was going to be blue-collar blacks and whites, the relic population of the river.

Back home, the fight was escalating. Armed with a tenacious lawyer, support from the neighboring Houmas House plantation and even the state attorney general's office, SOS entered the environmental hearings with a string of troubling questions. The waste site flooded in the spring. It was also on top of an aquifer than ran directly to the river, above the drinking water intakes for a half-dozen parishes downstream. Lurking in the background was the fear that the facility would begin importing toxic waste from other states, turning Louisiana into a kind of national waste pit. It was about this time that a soon-to-become-notorious garbage barge from Long Island was making its way south, looking for a dump site in the Louisiana coastal zone. An equally newsworthy freight train of frozen waste had come down from Tennessee and thawed out near the Louisiana border, spilling noxious liquids along the tracks. A floating commercial toxic waste incinerator with the daunting name Vulcanus was gearing up for a test run out of Lake Charles. And now we had IT.

The company need not to have worried. The state approved the permit. The state always granted permits. As one observer said at the time, the state environmental agency had "never met an industry it didn't like."

The Róberts went to court. The trial court, plainly vexed, agreed that the state had not answered basic questions about the operation, but left the permit in place. Undaunted, the Róberts soldiered on to the Supreme Court, where a miracle occurred. It reversed everything, and imposed a requirement that still leaves state agencies shaking their heads in dismay. Burnside might or might not be a good place for a hazardous waste site, the justices explained, but it was up to the state to examine all reasonable alternatives before making a decision. The ruling would be a deal killer. Nobody could contend that storing hazardous wastes in a floodplain along the Mississippi was the best idea around.

Following the court's decision, the IT project went back to the drawing board where, second miracle, it ran into a new governor who was not committed to the project. Instead, for one brief moment in Louisiana history, his people were green. They denied the IT permit.

You would know none of this story today, driving up River Road. The batture is on your left. The IT site is now a residential development called Pelican Point. The Cabin Restaurant is still there, and the floor of Teresa Róbert's kitchen still looks like the top of a cobbler's bench. State environmental agencies continue to treat industry as their client and the public as a latent and dangerous form of enemy whom it is best to keep at bay. But when things get really bad, there is also this Save Our Selves opinion lurking out there, also latent, potentially dangerous, and who knows who might bring it to court and challenge a particularly bad decision. It could happen.

That uncertainty is very helpful.

COMMUNIST

It is not every day that I get called a Communist, although down in south Louisiana the charge is made as earnestly as if Fidel might invade us tomorrow if only he could purchase the gas. It has been one of the corporate world's favorite words for environmentalists. Still, it was a little strange to find the C word out here on the batture, a place where no one who exercises more power over the river than to pee in it ever goes.

To begin with, you can hardly see this first patch of woods. It might take you five minutes to drive up River Road from the U.S. Army Corps of Engineers buildings, where the trees begin, to Ochsner Hospital and the power lines that make an end to them. Five minutes, that is, unless you get caught by a freight train crossing the road at the parish line, and the best you can do at this point is turn up the car radio because cursing them doesn't make them move any faster. I have tried that. It takes four engines to carry the big trains across the Mississippi at a height that will clear the passing tankers and cargo ships below. At least the railroad bridge was constructed in a straight line. The automobile bridge that accompanies it was built from both sides of the river towards the middle, enabling politicians to pay contractors on each bank. Only the contractors missed near the middle by a couple of feet. So you have to be alert up there on the Huey Long to a slight jog in the road, about a hundred feet in the air.

The first woods are hidden behind the levee. Off to the other side are auto garages, an abandoned dealership, some chain-linked lots, a power relay station, a bar—the usual aspect of the back side of town. Why the Mississippi River should be treated like the back side of anything has always puzzled me. People don't build their houses along this stretch in a way to observe the river, living instead at ground level in homes that, while well maintained, seem intended to avoid the most magnificent view in the American South. It is as if we were all afraid of it. The batture marks the high-water mark of a no-water mindset, the place where humans end. Every morning and evening thousands of commuters sealed in their automobiles crowd onto River Road traveling in and out of town, fleeing the city as if being caught here come sundown were like signing their death warrants. They, too, are afraid.

Then there are the other people. You can hop the levee here with ease because it is not topped by the concrete barriers that have given other levees around New Orleans the look of major prison facilities and their neighborhoods the feel of a siege. On the batture side and down into the woods is a collection of individuals whose composition changes daily. The blue tarp left over from a Katrina house may shelter a husband running from alimony, a Guatamalteco running from immigration, or a transient trying to make it cleaning motels out in Fat City, only the bus line stops up at Claiborne Avenue a mile walk from here and the bus ride takes him another hour and a quarter, one way. He tells me about it during the rains of January, sitting on a stained quilt with the seal of the Ambassador Hotel and surrounded by discarded bottles and potato chip bags. I met a fellow in here just before Mardi Gras who was killing a pint of bourbon and reading Ayn Rand. The next day I took him a Jimmie Lee Burke from the house but he had gone. A month later, the Ayn Rand was still there.

Schoolkids come down in the evenings, except for high summer when it stays hot in here until midnight and the mosquitoes are waiting. They come in groups of four or five to do the same things that the adults do, smoke cigarettes, pull on a beer, tell stories. At times they mix with the regulars, a bit uneasily, the adults up front by the fire and the kids in the rear, watching, asking few questions. They seem oddly respectful although these are clearly kids from well-off families taking a small walk on the wild side. The old hands open up with the youngsters around, expounding on whatever war we're engaged in, or, one evening on the merits of Vatican II. I move through slowly, talking to my dog, not wanting to horn in but not wanting to shun them either, catching their drift.

On this night, though, the kids are down by themselves. They have their own fire going, and, uninhibited by adults, their conversation has that school locker room ring, sharp declaratives followed by bursts of laughter. Someone who is not there, maybe a teacher, maybe a girl, is getting cut down.

My dog goes in first, towards the fire and the possibility of food. As Ms. Bear sees it, where there are people there is likely to be something to eat, and if looking black and cute doesn't work for her then there is always the possibility of something left on the ground. She has a bad stomach, however, so I come up close behind her, steering her past the flame, the boys on a log to the side, they quiet and waiting for me to leave. But instead of leaving, my dog goes over for a schmooze and they begin to pat her, looking at me, sizing me up warily as if maybe I am a policeman or even somebody their parents sent out to find them. They are smoking cigarettes, nothing stronger, and a can of something is down behind the log. Finding no food offers, the dog moves on, but as I turn, a voice follows me. "Don't I know you?"

I have never known what to do with a question like that so I don't say anything; I just turn and stand there, the firelight on their faces and mine. Then the boy says, "Aren't you on television?"

I say not really, but from time to time they might ask me a question about something. As I turn to leave, the boy calls out, "Wait, I know you, you're the Communist!"

Silence in the clearing. We are about twenty feet from the Mississippi River and the barges that are tied to the banks loom like tombs. The fire crackles and my dog has disappeared into the gloom. I am wondering where that question came from, and then it strikes me and I ask, "Does your father work for a law firm in town?"

The boy looks stunned, as if I had guessed his birthday. Maybe he understands what I am saying and maybe he doesn't, but I just say goodnight to them and go looking for the dog. In the dark of the night she is pure invisible.

A short while later Ms. Bear and I are topping the levee together and I am about to slip her leash on, because after you cross the railroad tracks the cars are deadly. But I am imagining the scene that must have taken place in that boy's house, some time before. His father, not a man to be trifled with, was home from the law firm and watching the evening news. On came a story about the environment, and then I appeared on the screen to say something unflattering about an industrial spill, maybe even his client. Daddy exploded. Goddamn Communist! And there was his boy taking it all in, a real communist, an ambassador of evil right here in New Orleans and they let him speak on television!

I wonder whether he will go home now and tell his father. It would be a risk. This is a secret place for boys, and his parents might not know about it. On the other hand, what a remarkable encounter.

SQUATTERS

THEY ARE OUT THERE EVERY MORNING TOGETHER, like ham and eggs, and he doesn't take them back in until after dark. There is a little plastic fire hydrant about two feet high, and a large plastic bowl of water. They are for you, or to be more accurate, unless you want to go down on your hands and knees, they are for your dog. The fellow who put them there will be in sight somewhere on the batture nearby, weeding a garden, cutting grass. He is one of the most tireless workers you will ever see. He lives in camp twelve of thirteen camps, homes really, on the batture side of the levee. Most of the camps stand on piles ten feet or so above the river, although at flood levels the water crawls into some of the lower ones and over the floors. They are the last homes on the batture between Baton Rouge and the Gulf of Mexico.

Rumor has it that there were "bad girls" up here who introduced many a local boy to the mysteries of nature, but I tended to discount them. They sounded like the elusive Swedish Bikini Team. Then I met a man who said that it was true but he wouldn't tell names. After two Bud Lights he told me the number of the camp and, some time later, the names of the girls. And the names of the sheriffs whose cars were always parked nearby. Now I don't know what to believe.

There was a time, of course, when most folks along the Mississippi lived on the batture or a stone's throw away from it. It was no idyll. No one loved this river more than Mark Twain, but what he reports seeing along the banks in the 1850s were "wretched little log cabins" with wood fences sticking a foot or two up out of the water and "one or two jeans-clad, chills-racked, yellow faced male miserables" on the top rail, "spitting tobacco through lost teeth," while the rest of the family rode it out with a few farm animals on a raft moored nearby. Huck Finn's father comes to mind. They hunkered down on America's batture frontier, owned no land, paid no taxes, and lived on whatever they could catch or came floating by. Strangers meant trouble. In south Louisiana, however, they found their final trouble with the Army Corps of Engineers.

In its defense, the Corps wanted nothing to do with levees or battures, to say nothing of batture people. Its job was to clear the lower Mississippi River for navigation and that was a handful right there. In the early days locals provided their own flood protection in the same way that they protected themselves from the rest of the elements. It took a series of bad flood years to force the Corps into the levee business, and even here only on the condition that they would be immune from lawsuits and that local governments would provide the rights of way. Which seemed straightforward enough, only the river would not cooperate. It kept moving back and forth, cutting into the right of way on one side and building it up on the other. Meanwhile flood stages kept on rising as the Corps busily straightened out the river's trajectory upstream. Here in New Orleans, the Corps had to adjust.

Over time, then, the engineers started building the levees larger and moving them back. The Carrollton area was particularly affected. New levees demolished the railroad station, with its stone front like the London Bridge, the Carrollton Hotel and Gardens, whose celebrated flowers, shooting galleries, cricket fields, bowling greens, regattas and dances drew weekend visitors year round, and the Carrollton landing where the *Cotton Blossom* came in on Friday evenings to perform *East Lynne*, a popular melodrama in which the audience was invited to encourage the heroine, cheer her swain, and throw fruit at the dark-suited villain. If you walk the levee top along its modern alignment, they are all on the river side now, buried under the batture trees and water.

The most difficult moving job of all, however, was the people. During the Great Depression, ad hoc settlements upstream of New Orleans began to boom. There was no rent to pay. These were not Mark Twain's style river people nor criminals on the lam, although some of these types doubtless floated up here. Nor were they mental cases, although the fellow who lived in a shipping box probably was, along with another one called St. John the Baptist who wrapped himself in a sheet and lay in wait to convert passersby. Most were hardworking folk down on their luck who found a niche on the east bank between Audubon Park upstream to the Jefferson Parish line and beyond.

They were squatters, nearly to a person. Some made their living in town as teachers, musicians, and auto mechanics. Some made their living running trotlines for catfish, setting shrimp traps, and making clothes poles from the willow trees. They dragged up old barges and salvaged the planks for siding. They went out in skiffs to snag firewood, too, looking for ash, which made the slowest and hottest burn, cutting the roots off with a short saw right there on the river, bucking up the logs on dry land. They would bring their catfish still squirming and their newly made furniture over the levee to the Carrollton market on Dante Street, hawking their wares with the rest of the street vendors; "WATERmelon!" and "CLOTHES-poles, mam!" Their kids went to the local schools. They played with the Oak Street boys in the riverside impoundments of the logging companies, jumping barefoot from trunk to trunk, follow the leader. Even Captain Bisso, the maritime king of the uptown area, lived on the batture. One of the batture houses went up three stories. Its neighbor was the Noah's Ark Baptist Church. Then, in the early 1950s, came the order to move.

It was an agony. Newspaper headlines tell the story: "Deadline to Quit Batture Is Fixed," "River Folks Are Saddened by Vacate Order of Board," "Batture People to Resist Order," "Dwellers Plan Batture Battle," "Batture People May Face Court," "Batture Homes Ordered Moved," "Deputies Give Batture Dweller the Bad News," "Engineers Still Pet Peeve of Aged Batture Man Facing Loss of Home,"

"Batture Tenants Pull Out; Bulldozers Going in Today," "Batture Clearance Starts; Dwellers Aided in Moving." It took about three years and then it was over, leaving so many personal stories behind. The "poet laureate" of the batture, seventy-three years old, refused to leave and had to be carried out by force. There are stories of moving the houses back with cooking fires still burning in the kitchen. Now they are gone, with the exception of thirteen camps above the parish line. These were the lucky ones. Jefferson Parish had managed to raise its levees in earlier years, so the Corps improvements stopped at the parish line, leaving these few standing.

So far. About a year ago on a weekend morning the occupants of these camps woke up to find metal no trespassing signs punched into their front lawns and driveways. The notices did not come from the levee board or the Corps this time. Instead they came from a grandson of the legendary Rudy O'Dwyer, Sr., he of the aviary and the Original Southport Club, who claims to own this piece of the batture. Ashton O'Dwyer has been trying to vindicate this legal claim since the early 1970s, so far without success, and the ups and downs of his journey resemble, in miniature, those of Edward Livingston two centuries ago. Maybe the batture dwellers hold titles from people who actually had title to the land. Maybe they have simply occupied O'Dwyer's land for long enough to defeat his claim. Another tangle for the courts to sort out. In the meantime, however, within hours of their posting most of the no trespassing signs had disappeared into the river. These batture folks are no more willing to leave than the last ones.

It is an odd assortment of houses up there right now, a neighborhood in transition. There are a few camps that look abandoned, although they are not. Their occupants must come out after midnight and get safely back in before dawn in the old river way, suspicious and perhaps with reason. One day someone might come and kick them out. In the early 1990s young couples began buying in and fixing up with lots of windows, wide porches, and river views. They would be your neighbors anywhere. One camp has been converted into a local lawyer's weekend party venue, and another has yielded to a small palace with double galleries that, landward of the levee, would start the bidding at half a million dollars. The trend here is upscale. The river roots of these dwellings will go. I do not know what is wrong with this picture, except that it is sad.

In the meantime, though, every time I go by, the man from camp twelve has the fire hydrant and the bowl of water out on the levee top and ready for a passing dog. His house is old-fashioned, low to the water, and neat as a pin. He is, of course, working, but when I wave he waves back. I'd hate like anything to lose him.

OIL

"You think the Atchafalaya is bad," he whispers to me. "Check out Chene, Boeuf, and Black."

I do not look at the man. We are standing next to each other in the men's room of the old Army Corps of Engineers building on top of the levee, a yellow, one-story complex that looks like an abandoned primary school. The accommodations of military establishments in those days had few niceties like separators between the urinals, so you got used to staring intently at the wall ahead of you as if it contained vital messages in small print, looking neither left nor right. Except, this man was talking to me. The etiquette here was challenging.

"It's a joke," the man says, walking to the washstand, and then he leaves the room. I feel like I am in a spy movie, or that Deep Throat has come to Louisiana, as in a dream. I've no idea what he was talking about. I am here, in the early 1970s, at the front end of a series of meetings over the future of the Atchafalaya floodway that would become more like a multiyear survivor show against the civilians in the engineering department, but I don't know that yet either. And along comes this man, a silent spectator at the meeting, telling me this tidbit about another channel project, below the floodway, where it empties into the Gulf of Mexico.

As it turned out, the Chene, Boeuf, and Black canals were a marvel of phantom economics and a death blow for the coast marshes around them. No matter. They provided free transit for two oil rig manufacturers, one of whom, I remember reading at the time, was found to have made over-the-limit campaign contributions to every member of the congressional delegation. I had stumbled over the oil industry in Louisiana and a whole new world where the Corps was not its own master, the state was not its own master, and even the delegation paid first homage to oil. One of President Carter's first acts in office was to try to stop the Chene, Boeuf, and Black project and others like it. He didn't stand a chance.

I'd first heard about the oil business in Louisiana from the oil business. I was working for the National Wildlife Federation in Washington, and we were concerned about Exxon drilling in the Everglades. Three attorneys for the corporation flew up from Houston to persuade us not to oppose the drilling. They were operating under strict conditions down there, they told us, as if the conditions were a terrible burden and Florida a tough cop on the beat. Searching for a convincing comparison, they added, "This isn't Louisiana, you know."

Back at the Atchafalaya meeting, we are taking a break. As much as anything else, we need to cut the tension in the room. I pour some coffee laced with a heart-stopping load of chicory and borrow a cigarette from a Corps employee, which promptly sets my head on fire. I tell myself that I am bonding, living down the stigma of being a Yankee from ten states away who knows nothing about Louisiana or the Corps and is down here to tell everybody what to do, which is not all that far from the case. We are outside now in the parking lot, watching the big boats go by to the petroleum plants upstream, proud achievements of a navigation network through coastal Louisiana that, at the time, only one or two scientists saw was destroying it, and they were treated like lepers. I go back to the men's room to rinse my face. There is a whole afternoon ahead, and we are not getting along very well.

It is not until years later, many meetings with hydrologists, classes in the marsh, that I began to realize that I'd been missing the big picture. Saving the Atchafalaya was a sideshow. All of south Louisiana was sinking under of a vast network of pipelines and canals. Just one of them, the Mississippi Gulf Outlet, having destroyed much of St. Bernard Parish, would usher Hurricane Katrina right into New Orleans. Out in the marsh, largely unseen except by fishing boats and then only in tiny pieces, were an additional five thousand miles of mini-canals to oil and gas sites, each one a rip through the living tapestry of the coast, death by five thousand blows. I wrote an article about it, and it was duly published and died.

It still dies. The state's coastal wetlands campaign, whose signature photo is an egret perched on a petroleum platform, is funded by Shell Oil and makes no mention of oil and gas harm to the zone. Nor does the Shell exhibit at the aquarium downtown, which features fish around an oil rig. The state and the oil and gas industry have joined forces to persuade Congress that the American taxpayer should pay to put our Humpty Dumpty back together again. No suggestion is made of a contribution from the industry, the largest member of which cleared thirty-six billion dollars in profits last year, with four others close behind. And whose major damage here, by this late date, is uncontestable. Instead, Shell sponsors Jazz Fest.

Enter Mr. Bill. He entered my office, in fact, a year or so ago, an unprepossessing artist from the French Quarter who launched a popular sketch on *Saturday Night Live* featuring a puppet figure and his companions, the World of Mr. Bill. I'd not seen it, which seemed to disappoint him, but he had other things on his mind, a program on the coast. Would I participate? Sure, I said. He had some video he wanted me to see. We plugged it in. It covered a recent forum here in New Orleans on the disappearing coast, featuring one of our two senators and other luminaries. Platitudes sprayed from the podium like water from a lawn sprinkler, the situation was grave, the price tag would be steep, we must work together. Then came questions from the audience. A man, who looked from the back like our artist from the Quarter, stood up and asked what plans existed for the oil and gas industry to help pay the bill. Dead silence. The camera panned the panelists. The senator, a nice person in every way, looked pole-axed, struck by the Strange Question from Mars. The moderator coughed and asked whether any member of the panel wished to reply to the questions. But he was laughing. He knew that no one did. And no one did.

This past spring a tiny biplane flew over the Jazz Fest crowds, trailing the message, SHELL—HEAR THE MUSIC—FIX THE COAST U BROKE. Sponsored by Mr. Bill. Not many people looked up, but Shell was taking no chances. A young man handing out leaflets outside the entrance gate was handcuffed and hustled away by the police. The beloved funk pianist Dr. John was not hustled away. He had told the newspaper the week before that he was tired of the oil industry ripping off the coast and wanted to speak up about it. "Shell and their friends in the industry don't think they owe us anything," Dr. John said. "We got to let them know we're hip to them." A few days later he said that his comments had been misinterpreted.

And so it is that south Louisiana may sink into the Gulf of Mexico with hymns to the oil industry on its lips, never making the connection between the two. Many years ago, new to the state, I attended the Mardi Gras celebration in Washington, D.C. The ballroom was jammed with politicians, lobbyists, developers, and other favor seekers, under the banner of that year's theme: "Louisiana Naturally." Several hours of drinks, business, and finger food finally yielded to the main event, the presentation of the Queens. Spotlights lit up the stage, and out came the selected daughters of assembly, each dressed in a white, off-the-shoulder gown reminiscent of *Gone with the Wind*. On top of which, they carried little oil rigs. Looking back, they seem a kind of metaphor.

TIME

You can set your watch by them, they come so regularly each evening, 6:30 on the dot, wave after wave, as few as three or four and as many as fifty in a flight, the three or four seeming to make up for their numbers with even louder shrieks and cries, the whistling ducks coming home. For twenty frantic minutes the sky is full of them and then it goes silent again; they have safely passed. The other night I fixed a line of ten birds in my mind and began counting. By 6:50 they were at 1,290. In just my part of the sky.

It seemed like a tremendous amount. The next day, however, while researching for a class, I came across a description of a flight of passenger pigeons by a nineteenth-century ornithologist who, upriver on the Mississippi, described being "struck with astonishment" by a roaring sound and instant darkness. As he was rushing outside, a young boy told him, "It is only the pigeons." The boy was already preparing his nets and clubs to kill them, "twenty or thirty dozen in a sweep." The ornithologist, Alexander Wilson, did some quick math. Supposing the column to be one mile wide (and he believed it to be considerably more) and moving at the rate of one mile a minute, for four continuous hours, three birds per square yard, he came to 2,230,272,000 birds. In that one event. The nets and clubs proved to be quite effective. Cutting down their roosting trees turned out to be even more effective. I have an old sketch of the passenger pigeon, below which the caption tells us that "there is no zoo or ornithological garden in which this species is wanting." The last one on earth died in the St. Louis zoo in 1914.

So exactly what is a tremendous amount of birds? The 1,290 whistlers I'd counted barely merited a look skyward one hundred-plus years ago. Our baselines shift. I remember visiting a friend in New York City last year. The haze from the traffic obscured the sun like a thin fog and the smell of exhaust was pervasive, but at the noon hour every square inch of available outdoor space was occupied by secretaries and executives in dresses and shirtsleeves, smiling, faces to the sky, exclaiming to each other, "What a beautiful day!" For them it was. They had forgotten what honest-to-God sunlight looked like and the smell of fresh air. Pollution was the new normal. I find myself wondering whether that is bad or good. Imagine the unhappiness of those New Yorkers if, magically, one were to replace their air and sky with the real deal, sharp and clean, and then, after they appreciated the difference, just as magically one made it disappear again, returning them to today. I wonder whether we are better off knowing these things or not knowing them.

I am airing this thought with my friend Tim, a former student, down under the power lines. I had come early to sit on a bank of sand and a light a small fire of driftwood, carefully keeping my sneakers from the flame. I have several pairs of athletic shoes at home with their soles curled off from the heat; some things I know but I never learn. For a while I watched a fringe of cloud move slowly upriver, pretty as a petticoat and edged with neat ruffles that ran the entire width of the sky. From the other direction, against the clear and darkening blue, came the contrail of a jet airplane, its silver body ahead like a projectile, its path straight and inexorable as a pistol shot, directly at the petticoat cloud. It was going to be terrible. The plane streaked through the cloud, and at that very moment the petticoat began to fall apart, disaggregating into patches and then shreds and thin lines. The plane had won. How could it not. It is what humans do.

As dark fell, Tim appeared, and soon behind him a line of four young men in jeans and sweatshirts who edged the beach towards the bank downstream where a large barge lay at anchor, and had lain at anchor for years. Tim had brought some beers, a brand I'd never heard of, but there were so many new brands these days that perhaps someone was simply pasting on new labels, and as we opened them I noticed the lead youngster climbing towards a barge on a set of tires that surrounded the anchor post like a bumper. The tires were unsteady climbing, sagging underfoot, but he made it, and soon he was standing on top of them, eyeballing a six-foot gap of water between him and the deck of the vessel. He tried leaning out to the deck but it was out of reach. A tie rope ran from the anchor to a cleat on the deck, but it looked loose and sagging. I could see the boy crouching, measuring a leap, and I thought I should do something here but I could not think of exactly what, and then, the young man disappeared. I heard no shouts of alarm, however, and assumed that he had simply given up and jumped back down.

When I next glanced downriver, to my surprise the boy was on the deck of the barge, and a second one had mounted the tires, taking his turn. He, too, hesitated, then disappeared, and then reappeared at the rim of the barge, crawling over it, getting to his feet, triumphant. The last two followed. They walked to the front of the barge and sat down in a circle; they were only shadows now, lit from behind by the lights from the granaries and a loading ship across the way. The river was black and sparkled with little flames. Tim and I got to thinking about how much one would pay for a ringside dinner on the Mississippi River on such a night, the big water stretching down to the lights of the city and upstream to the Huey Long bridge with its rivulet of the headlights of tiny cars. He said, for a good serving in Los Angeles, maybe two, three hundred dollars. More, if they didn't rush you. Out here on the river, there was no rush.

How amazing it would be to have lived at a time when the only lights on the river were fires from squatters' camps and the boats passing by, and when the ducks passed overhead so thick that their wind tossed your clothes. I asked Tim the question that nearly everyone in New Orleans, tied so closely to history, asks at one moment or another, would I rather have lived back then? The proposition is as impossible to imagine as it is to resist thinking about, because no sane person would want to run the gauntlet of disease and sudden calamity that haunted this region, but still. Nor could one willingly enter the violence, racism, and huckster ballyhoo that accompanied, in their time, the spectacular abundance of nature not yet imperiled by man. But still. If I knew what I know now, I told Tim, I could not abide it. And if I did not know what I know now, then I might not abide that either. We concluded that we'd like to go visit. With a stash of antibiotics of course.

The conversation trailed off. I fed some more sticks into the fire. It was not a cold evening, but there are things about a fire that have little to do with keeping warm. We heard noises from downstream and noticed the four young men preparing to leave the barge and come ashore. Watching closely for their technique now, but blinded by the darkness, I only saw them disappear from the deck, reappear on the tires, and climb down. On their way out they passed near our fire this time, and I recorded that they had unusually long hair, and full hips, and finally it dawned on me that they were young women, not men at all. I had seen jeans, sweatshirts, and most of all a feat of derring-do boarding the barge, added to the fact that I rarely saw young women down here and never at night, and had drawn an entirely wrong conclusion.

I said good evening to them as they came by, and when one replied, I said, could I ask you how you made the move to the barge? The one in the lead said, easy. There was the tie rope and a wire below it. You stood on the wire like a tight rope, held onto the tie rope, and shuffled across. Across the water, I am thinking, which was dark and black underneath, and ran under the bottom of the barge.

What would I say if I knew that my daughter was doing this? I would be scared, and proud too, I suppose. When they had left, I told Tim that something wonderful had just happened. He turned to me and said, there's your answer, Prof. That's why you can't go back.

But still. I continue to wrestle with the question of time. I do not mean the opportunity to relive my life, as in would I want to be younger again, but instead about a different baseline. Perhaps the saddest thing I can think of is that my children will accept a new normal without the wonderful things that I took for normal, now gone. Which presents another dilemma: what to tell them.

When Lisa and I moved to New Orleans, thirty years ago, we packed up our little car, towed a small U-Haul, stowed the boys in the backseat like raccoons, and drove all day until we reached Knoxville, frazzled and ready to crash. There were at least ten motel options at the route 40 exit, but we chose Howard Johnson's because somewhere back in childhood we remembered twenty-seven flavors of ice cream. Our room was on the top floor, and the boys, age six and three, rushed to be the first to unlock the door. On the far side of the room was the standard plate glass window, covered with a drape that they managed to open by pulling, together, on a cord. There below us, beyond the window, shone the most awesomely ugly scene imaginable in a country untouched by war.

The entire landscape was paved, horizon to horizon, one large parking lot feeding into multiple fast-food, Jiffy Stop, and similar services, each of which had a neon sign larger than the other. I remember a Roy Rogers with an illuminated, blinking lariat and a Sno-Cone that spilled huge drops of vanilla towards the ground. There were no trees. There was no grass. There wasn't even a place to walk. Yellow, red, and green lights from the franchises pulsed against the motel room walls. Our younger boy turned to his older brother in awe. "Cyp!" he said, "isn't it *beautiful?*" The older, also smitten but a little more cautious, turned to me for affirmation. I was staring at that landscape as if I were seeing the gates of Hell.

Here I was at a new baseline. I could tell them something I did not believe at all, that it looked beautiful indeed, and my boys would be happy. Or I could say what I really felt, very deeply, and cut a wound in them that might last for life, as mine has. I could see Lisa looking at me, shaking her head.

MALORIE

One spring while I was away, Lisa took to bringing our dog to the batture, and soon she found her own sweet spot down here, a place she only recently showed me. If you wander upriver from the power lines, past the little batture houses, past an equipment graveyard with rusting truck bodies, jaws from river dredges, and oil retention booms, you come to a longer line of woods that runs up to the Huey Long Bridge and miles beyond. Well before the bridge is a set of barges banked against the batture like a buffer, five and six deep. I've never seen them moved. My guess is that this is their final resting place, chosen because the river here takes a sharp bend, and the force of high water, piling in, could threaten the levees behind. The barges also protect a rise of batture trees, cut off by a muddy slough to their rear. I'd always swung out along the levee when walking by this stretch. I'd never gone in to investigate.

It is an ominous place, even on a sunny day. The overhead trees are thick and block the light, the barges form a wall to the left, and to the right is an arm of stagnant water. The levee seems miles away. It is utterly silent here, only the peep of a distant bird. About a quarter mile in you notice, on the other side of the slough, away from the river, a wrecked and gutted barge lying at an angle with tall willow trees rising from its innards. Beyond it is another, in a line, and farther down the bow of yet another still. They are huge, and silent, a former wall of defense, and they speak of death as plainly as a graveyard. Only this graveyard is open, above ground, and you can see nature eating away the carcasses and pushing up new shoots from within.

I have been up here several times since Lisa first brought me, and every time, knowing what is coming, I am still subdued and a little shocked by these open vaults, the living consuming the long deceased. They served their purpose, nobly, one could say. Still, it is not an explanation that brings dead things to life.

A little farther on, there is an opening where you can walk down to the river by the new barge line. Which is not to say that these barges are new, either. The ones nearest the shore have been out of service a long time, and show large rips in their hulls. At low water, the sand flat along them is smooth and easy walking. Picking our way forward, we are suddenly stopped by a blue stegosaurus, life sized, painted perfectly on the side of a barge. Beyond it, a double-headed monster is saying something, only it is written in what my son tells me is gang language, all swirls and colors, as undecipherable as Arabic and just as intricately patterned. But it is the next barge that holds the prize.

On one entire side is the face of a lovely, green-eyed woman, smiling, perfect white teeth, red lips, seen through the shape of a purple butterfly. To her left is a smaller butterfly in orange and black, clearly a monarch, and above her head is the silhouette of a live oak tree, brooding. At the other end of this barge, peeking between two anchor pilings, is a ten-foot face of Donald Duck, beak open and quacking. These paintings reach fifteen feet in the air. I see no spray cans, no scaffolding, and no ladder. Whoever did this brought all of the gear in over the levee, down through the woods, past the old ghost barge wall, fording the slough, to these barges at the river's edge. And then took it out again the same way.

A week later we go back. It is a December day, cloudy and breezy, and we are looking for niches where birds might feed. There is not much moving in here, but when we drop down along the barges we are surprised to see new painting. The green-eyed woman has turned into a mural, and opposite her face, fully the same dimension, is an inscription in black gothic lettering against a lavender background. "Malorie," it says, followed by "RIP" and the dates, "1986–2007." She was twenty-one years old. Someone I will never see or know has come down to this end of the earth to paint her memorial. A mural that no one else is ever likely to see, because no one else ever comes this way. There is no path. The woods dead-end into the river. I mean, what are the odds of my wife and the dog happening by?

I am as taken as I was by the motorcycle in the woods downriver by Cooter Brown's. Most people draw, paint, and write for other people. They cannot wait to show what they have done. It is the same for people who make a great deal of money, I suppose; what is the use of making it if nobody else knows it? But here is this other mindset, a creativity so selfless and instinctual that it brings these artists to these lonely spots to do their works, not to be seen, but almost in order *not* to be seen. Perhaps not, though, else they would have then destroyed them afterwards. Perhaps rather, for these rare and gifted people there is the simple fact that the batture provides sanctuary. Out here, nobody is going to tell them no.

It is cold out, my wife and the dog have moved away, but I stand in front of Malorie and take my cap off. I feel a little ridiculous, but it is the only way I can think of to pay my respects.

DOG

I AM SHELTERED AGAINST A LOG, grading papers. To my left a thicket of willows juts up like a haircut and to my right is the Mississippi, blocked from view by huge outfall pipes from the New Orleans water system. Every once in a while a gush of brown sludge spills out into the river, sediments from a filtering pond about a half mile uptown. Ahead of me as on a movie screen is the full width of the water, boats going up and down, huge tankers the length of a city block and rafts of eight barges at a time, pushed from the rear by tugs whose pilothouses sit up like towers and fit into the rear of the raft like plugs in a socket.

I let my mind wander. It cannot be easy to steer these beasts. Every once in a while an ocean-going vessel misreads the near-shore eddy and grounds on the batture like a stranded whale. One unfortunate ship called the *Bright Star* lost its bearings in downtown New Orleans and slammed into the Riverwalk. By some miracle it killed no one, but gave rise to several Krewe de Vieux floats the following Mardi Gras, one of them a cut-out rowboat held up by a crew that ran along yelling, "Look out!" and crashing into buildings along Frenchman Street. It turned out that the *Bright Star* was steered by a Chinese captain who spoke no English, under the guidance of an American pilot who spoke no Chinese.

The real mysteries, though, are the long barge rafts that are steered entirely by the force of the tug's twin motors in the rear, the pilot cutting back on one motor or the other to make a turn. Which takes some anticipation, that far back in the stern. Turning the bow even on a long canoe is a chore. Tows on the Mississippi can run up to three hundred feet, all payload, out ahead of you like a warehouse.

Then there is the question of who is in the wheelhouse and whether or not he is awake. Louisiana's record oil spill in 2008 came about when a tanker sliced through a barge that had, inexplicably, cut directly across its path, mid-river. The slick closed down the lower Mississippi for a week. It turns out that the tugboat pushing the barge was being piloted by a young apprentice with no solo experience on the river, and whose schedule had required him to be up and working for the previous three days without relief. The tug's captain, whose presence on board was said to be mandatory, had taken off for Illinois to see his girlfriend. At a subsequent hearing he explained that a cousin had called to alert him that his girlfriend had been seen with another man. A perfectly Louisiana excuse.

I go back to grading exams. Ms. Bear is by me in a nest of sand against the log, warming in the winter sun. She is getting old now, and when she reaches the batture she wants to run but pulls up lame. We can no longer walk over here anymore. I have to drive over and shepherd her in. There will come a morning when she does not get up because she is no longer breathing, and I already know what I will do. I will carry her here and bury her in the willows. It is probably illegal, although from time to time I see other little gravesites for someone's pet in these batture woods, small markers and plastic flowers. I will leave no marker. But I will like thinking of her in this place where we have been together for so many years, she skipping up the waterline with her nose in the flotsam, sniffing out stray pieces of corn from the granaries upstream or, her lucky day, a catfish skin.

My mind drifts again. Lisa has come to love this dog, but at first sight it was quite otherwise. I had been out with my students in the Atchafalaya swamp and starting home, night falling, the car ahead of me stopped for a white dog in the road. There was not a house in sight, not even a light, and so the student driving scooped the dog into his car and drove on. As I was about to follow, a movement at the side of the road caught my eye, and I saw something I thought was a squirrel, tiny, mangy, and dark. It was not a squirrel; it was a puppy maybe a month old and it clearly was not at the top of its game. One side had no hair. It seemed to walk sideways. I picked it up, got back into the car, stuck it between my legs like you are not supposed to do with a hot cup of coffee, and drove on, fully intending to turn this creature over to the first bidder at the next gas stop. Something different happened. On the way, less than a thirty-minute drive, feeling the warmth between my thighs, the little muzzle poking out, the breathing, I knew there was no way I was going to give this thing away.

I arrived home late that evening, later than usual from one of these trips which are always late, and walked into the house with the dog in a towel, under one arm. Lisa appeared from the kitchen. You have to understand her perspective here. She had just finished raising two boys, while working, while I was out doing this and that, and she was on the verge of sending her second one off to college. A window of freedom lay ahead. And in I walk with a dog. She said to me, "What is that?" Now, of course, she knew exactly what it was. What she had just asked me was not a question at all. I promised her that I would find a student to take the dog at the earliest opportunity. I might have meant it, I can't remember.

What followed was shameful. The fact is, many students heard by the grapevine that I had picked up a puppy and a small parade of them filed by to ask whether I would give it away. I appeared willing, just wanted to ask a few questions, such as did they have a yard for the dog to play in, and would they be able to walk it several times a day, had they thought of the costs of shots and veterinary care, how about the weekend social life, and what were they going to do next summer, perhaps travel to another city, and where did the dog fit in those plans? I would sadly report back to Lisa and to my son Gabriel who was still home at the time, both very much cat people, that I was having difficulty finding qualified owners. We don't want to turn this dog over to just anyone, I said. Meanwhile, the dog had started to chew the furniture.

I didn't name her. A neighbor boy came by one day and, seeing the dog, called it a bear. She became Ms. Bear, and who in the world would get rid of a dog called Ms. Bear? The question was never stated, but it hung over the household like a blimp. Eventually, the dog won. It was never declared, she just stayed. She stopped chewing things, and I sanded down and refinished the ones she had as best I could. She started sleeping upstairs. One night she came up on the bed to sleep, and that was that.

Thirteen years ago now, I am thinking, watching her breathe in her pocket in the sand. The sun is on her flank, which is rising and falling. Out beyond us a large boat has passed, its waves lapping against the shore. They will subside. But another will come, until it too subsides.

HIGHEST AND BEST

IT IS SUMMER AGAIN, and the high water has been receding so slowly that the woods below the power lines still bottom on soft mud, criss-crossed by the tracks of either a herd of wild pigs or one of them on pharmaceuticals. The only human prints are my own as the mud tries to suck off my shoes and claim them for its own. The place has been swept clean by the high water, several years of accumulated beer cans, plastic bags, old tarps, and miscellaneous clothing that humans seem compelled to leave behind. We are the animal that trashes. The river is the animal that comes along and washes it away.

Passing by Cooter Brown's, I look up the Carrollton leg of the trolley line, shaded by live oak trees that go back before the time of anyone living today. In the 1960s, when the interstate highway came through town, the big idea was to get rid of these trees in the name of progress for a four-lane extension to the river. Mildred Fossier, then head of the city's parks and parkways, put her job on the line opposing it, announcing to the press that she would charge the Department of Streets one hundred and forty thousand dollars per tree. There are times that passion wins. I thank Mildred, passing by.

Upstream, past the horse stables and the batture houses, past the Huey Long Bridge, the trees between us and the river yield to a long stretch of open pits, dug out for the sand. Dump trucks roll in and out to feed the appetite of a region built on sinking soils and prone to deny it with street signs like Hillcrest Oaks (below sea level, no oaks) and, my favorite, Mount Rushmore Drive. I recently came across a real estate advertisement for the sale of this batture property back in the 1980s, several thousand feet along the river. The ad said that its intended use as a sand pit and barge docks was the "highest and best use" of the property, as evidenced by the cash flow it produced. Edward Livingston, arguing for his piece of the batture two hundred years ago, would agree.

The same day that I came across this advertisement, I also discovered the story of Papa Dukie & The Mud People. Up the Mississippi, not far, is the river town of Wallace, Louisiana, ringed by sugarcane, industrial plants, and the big river levee. One day in the early 1970s two busloads of hippies gassed up in Wallace, took a look around, and decided to go over the levee and camp on the batture. Led by Eddie "Duke" Edwards, a professional drummer coming home to Louisiana, they were musicians and they would jam all night. They were also cooks and crafts makers, and soon they were serving food and selling tie-dyed T-shirts to the locals. Worse, it was said that the hippie girls were daubing themselves with mud and swimming naked in the river, which struck fear in the hearts of law-abiding citizens. They sent the sheriff out to investigate. Whatever he found and saw he must have enjoyed, because Papa Dukie and the mud people stayed. Until they suddenly left, with the wind, as those years did, too.

Was theirs a "lower and worse" use? I think about Ricky and his friends, the teenagers who sneak down to smoke cigarettes and try the sour taste of their first beers, and the kids on their dirt bicycles, the ones coming out in wet cutoffs from the sand pit ponds, the ones on rope swings, and the ones who build forts on the riverbank and tree huts from washed-up logs and doors. Here run the dogs, the wild pigs, and the rabbits, and even the men who chase after them with golf clubs. Here is this accidental space, long, green, and much too thin. A smarter plan would have been to set the river levees farther back and give the Mississippi some space, but that chance came and went. Exactly what space we do have is here, and where it is headed has never been articulated.

The batture, of course, is as unaware of this question as a barn-yard chicken. Were it a more stable place, a more beautiful place, it would have been gobbled up a long time ago. Scruffy, unglamorous, and prone to flooding, it has a better chance of surviving. There are times high water can be your very good friend.

I hear thunder to the west. At any moment it could rain down from a clear blue sky.

ACKNOWLEDGMENTS

A BOOK LIKE THIS COMES FROM MANY PEOPLE, some of whom I've seen over the years out on the levee and have never known by name. Others like Ricky, Paggio, and Alcide Verret have contributed their part just by living out their lives on batture ground. Still others took the time to sit with me and tell their stories in much richer detail than I could capture here. They include Mildred Fossier, who told me about a childhood evening when she was peeping into a church off the batture while a preacher rocked the congregation with the awaiting terrors of hell, when a sudden crash of thunder came so close it seemed to fulfill the prophesy and sent everyone fleeing into the night; Connie, the bicycle man who still rides down the levee to watch the fishermen and who in his youth would row out in his skiff with his "two whores," as he says, making rowing motions with his hands, being sure I get the pun; Louis Otto, a skilled wood carver who grew up on Oak Street by the levee and performed antics with his young buddies in front of the new plate-glass window of the jewelry store; Ashton O'Dwyer, who told me about the Original Southport Club, the aviary on Monticello Street, and the sixteen-cylinder Cadillac in his grandfather's garage; Vic Landry, who has been in the New Orleans levee business for more than thirty years and told me about the the old Corps buildings with their waste pipes to the river; Joan Exnicios, the official river navigator for the lower Mississippi, who provided me with narratives of the Ames Crevasse; Larry Powell, a Tulane historian who lent me his interview with Ellis Marsalis on the old Marsalis Motel; Rich Campanella, a historian and cartographer who led me to reports on the slave insurrections; and Sigrid Bonner, a former student who lived on the levee and with whom I have mused that, after all, we are all on borrowed ground here in southern Louisiana, the batture of our lives.

In addition, I need to recognize the work of Jane Johnston, who assisted in the preparation of this manuscript and drew the designs for several chapter headings. Lastly, I would like to acknowledge the patience of my wife Lisa, who has come to accept my batture wanderings as a part of our rhythm, of my son Cyprian, who has developed a keener eye for birds, and of my son Gabriel, who, in a much better story of his own, inspired me to write this book. I would also include my dog, Ms. Bear, were she able to read. On the other hand, her sense of smell is uncanny.

SOURCES

Property

p. 10 Spanish and French traditions ... : Charles Sherman, *Roman Law in the Modern World* (Boston: Boston Book Company, 1917), p. 141.

p. 10 The civil code declared ... : Ari Kelman, *A River and Its City: The Nature of Landscape in New Orleans* (Berkeley and Los Angeles: University of California Press, 2003), p. 24.

p. 10 But in the late ... : Carleton Hunt, *Life and Services of Edward Livingston*, address on the occasion of the annual meeting of the Louisiana Bar Association, May 9, 1903, in the Chamber of the Supreme Court of the State of Louisiana, New Orleans, J. G. Hauser, 1903, pp. 3, 17.

p. 10 Edward Livingston was about ... : Henry Rightor, "Edward Livingston," *Standard History of New Orleans* (Chicago: Lewis Publishing Company, 1900), pp. 406–7.

p. 10 He was an accidental ... : Kelman, *A River*, pp. 28–29.

p. 10 He remade himself, adding ... : Hunt, pp. 124–25.

p. 10 Livingston's accomplishments in the ... : www.1911enyclopeia.org/Edward_Livingston, Classic Encyclopedia Brittanica.

p. 10 Indeed, Livingston declined ... : Merrill Peterson, "Sage of Monticello," *Thomas Jefferson and the New Nation* (New York: Oxford University Press, 1970), pp. 944–45.

p. 10 Instead, if he won ... : Ibid., p. 944.

p. 10 The American notion of ... : Ibid.

p. 11 By precedent rising from ... : Thomas Jefferson, *The Writings of Thomas Jefferson: Inaugural Addresses and Messages* (New York: Derby & Jackson, 1859), pp. 515, 517.

p. 11 In a city oppressed ... : H. C., "The New Orleans Levee: The Natural Results of Natural Causes," *New York Times*, December 2, 1879.

p. 11 When Livingston's client undertook ... : Hunt, p. 140.

p. 11 He went out a ... : Peterson, p. 945.

p. 11 On the other was . . . : Kelman, *A River*, p. 24.

p. 11 Thomas Jefferson considered the . . . : Ibid.

p. 11 After Livingston won his . . . : Hunt, p. 141.

p. 11 at which point Livingston . . . : Frederick Hicks, *Men and Books Famous in the Law* (Rochester, N.Y.: The Lawyers Co-Operative Publishing Company, 1921; reprinted 2000 by Beard Books), p. 167.

p. 11 When the dust settled . . . : Ibid., p. 168.

p. 11 Compromise that it was . . . : Kelman, *A River*, p. 49.

p. 11 New Orleanians not only . . . : Ibid., p. 44.

p. 11 He and Robert Fulton . . . : Tom Lewis, "The Democratic River," *The Hudson: A History* (New Haven, CT: Yale University Press, 2005), p. 157.

p. 12 Fulton's steamboat had one . . . : The following paragraph is as described in Kelman, *A River*, p. 50.

p. 12 Henry Shreve came from . . . : Ari Kelman, "Forests and Other River Perils," in Craig Colten, ed., *Transforming New Orleans and Its Environs* (Pittsburgh: University of Pittsburgh Press, 2000), pp. 49–50.

p. 12 He built his own . . . : Kelman, *A River*, pp. 57–58.

p. 12 Now Shreve had actually . . . : Kelman, "Forests," pp. 49–50.

p. 12 More threatening, Shreve tried . . . : Ibid.

p. 12 Livingston had to make . . . : The following paragraph is as described in Kelman, *A River*, p. 59; see also Hodding Carter, *Lower Mississippi* (New York: Farrar and Rinehart, 1942), pp. 219–21 (describing the Shreve-Livingston standoff). Livingston is reported to have told Shreve, "You deserve well of your country, young man, but we shall be compelled to beat you if we can." Ibid., p. 221.

p. 12 Two hundred years later . . . : Mark Waller, "Batture Property Rights in Question," *Times-Picayune*, May 29, 2007, http://blog.nola.com/topnews/2007/05/fishers_endure_odyssey_to_ply.html.

p. 12 Out near Lake Pontchartrain . . . : "Lake Pontchartrain and Vicinity: Status of Tree Removal Program," http://www.mvn.usace.army.mil/hps2/images/Survey_ROE_map.jpg.

High Water

p. 15 Pesticides managed to eliminate . . . : Michael Lipske, "How Rachel Carson Helped Save the Brown Pelican," *National Wildlife*, December/January 2000, vol. 38, no. 1.

p. 15 The whistling ducks are . . . : John Patton O'Neill, *Great Texas Birds*, edited by Suzanne Winckler (Austin: University of Texas Press, 1999), p. 24.

p. 15 is all one . . . : See statement of oncologist Dr. Carl G. Kardinal, Ochsner Foundation Hospital, Metairie, Louisiana: "No one really knows what is happening to the water in the Mississippi River. . . . No one knows for sure what these chemicals are doing in the Mississippi River as far as cancer is concerned."

Shoenberger, "Survey Will Probe High Cancer Rate in Area," *Times-Picayune*, Aprril 15, 1982. See also statement of of EPA chemist Eugene Sawicki: "It's human experimentation going on . . . all we can do right now is collect statistics from our human guinea pigs so to speak, then wait and see." Michaud, "Three Plant Areas under Federal Study," *Sunday Advocate*, February 18, 1979. Research by Dr. Marise Gottlieb of the Tulane University School of Medicine, M. Gottlieb et al., "Cancer and Drinking Water in Louisiana: Colon and Rectum," 1981, and Dr. Pelayo Corryea of the LSU School of Medicine, cited in Sierra Club, Delta Chapter, "Emissions of 212 Pounds of Toxic Chemicals into the Air in the Saint Gabriel/Geismar Area," 1986, showed rectal cancers at more than twice the normal elevations for those living along the Mississippi River, and a 60 percent greater chance of lung cancer. To which a Louisiana Chemical Association representative responded, "I'm tired of having to address the issue of cancer and the chemical industry, when there is no evidence that they are related." "Industry, Cancer Link Unproved," *Morning Advocate*, April 25, 1985, quoting LCA President Fred Loy. The 2008 Environmental Protection Agency inventory ranks the state of Louisiana fifth in toxic water discharges, the vast majority of them from plants along the Mississippi River. EPA, Toxic Release Inventory, p. B-11. If discharges from the mining industry are subtracted, Louisiana leads the nation. Ibid., pp. B-11, B16a. Louisiana colon and rectal cancer rates continue to lead the nation as well (fifth in death ratios for white males, first for black males). Cancer in Louisiana 2001–2005, LSU Health Sciences Center, vol. 23, fig. 3. Louisiana ranks second in the country in overall cancer rates, National Cancer Institute, Cancer Mortality Maps & Graphs available at http://cancercontrolplanet.cancer .gov/atlas/index1.jsp?.ac=1.

p. 16 "screw too much . . .": "Great Louisiana Toxics March Sets the Pace for the Movement," *Rachel's Hazardous Waste News* #101, October 31, 1988, quoting from a story in the *Washington Post*.

p. 16 zone at its mouth . . . : Press release, "Spring Nutrient Delivery to the Gulf Estimated among the Highest in Three Decades," *US Geological Survey*, July 11, 2008.

p. 16 Granted, a lot of . . . : "Mississippi river water quality and the Clean Water Act" by National Academies Press, National Research Council (U.S.). Committee on Animal Nutrition, p. 54, available at http://books.google.com/books?id=INww kzzIOtwC&pg=PP1&dq=mississippi+river+water+quality+and+the+clean+ water+act.

p. 16 The heavy metals and carcinogens, though . . . : Greenpeace, *We All Live Down-stream: The Mississippi River and the National Toxics Crisis*, December 1989, p. 91.

p. 16 130 industrial plants . . . : Ibid.

p. 17 state issues a report . . . : "Louisiana Tumor Registry: About LTR," http:// publichealth.lsuhsc.edu/tumorregistry/about_LTR.asp.

p. 17 state will not disclose . . . : "Louisiana Tumor Registry: Requests for Data," http://publichealth.lsuhsc.edu/tumorregistry/data_request.asp.

Spillway

p. 24 The Bonnet Carré spillway . . . : "Final Environmental Impact Statement, U.S. Army Corps of Engineers, Mississippi River and Tributaries Levee and Channel Improvement," February 1976, pp. 43–44.

p. 24 it resisted the notion . . . : John Barry, *Rising Tide* (New York: Touchstone, 1998), pp. 32–92.

p. 24 Not until 1927 when . . . : "Final Environmental Impact Statement," pp. 3, 4; Barry, pp. 423–26.

p. 24 on the Atchafalaya River . . . : Martin Reuss, *Designing the Bayous: The Control of Water in the Atchafalaya Basin, 1800–1995* (College Station: Texas A&M University Press, 2004); John McPhee, *The Control of Nature* (New York: Farrar, Straus, and Giroux, 2003), pp. 3–92.

p. 25 an international jetport in . . . : Matt Scallan, "Nagin Will Propose New Site for Airport," *Times-Picayune*, May 17, 2005, p. 1.

p. 25 airport in Lake Pontchartrain . . . : Dennis Pessica, "Eastern N.O. Airport Study on Turbulent Course," *Times-Picayune*, December 1, 1993, p. A9; Kim Chatelain, "New Airport Won't Fly, Critics Say," *Times-Picayune*, December 2, 1993, p. A-8.

p. 25 You don't understand, he . . . : Personal conversation with New Orleans mayor Barthelemy, November 1993, accompanied by Dr. Robert Thomas, who at the time directed the Louisiana Nature Center in New Orleans East.

p. 25 the wave of Florida-style . . . : Interview with Willie Fontenot, former member, Office of the Attorney General, Louisiana, June 30, 2009; Mr. Fontenot was a member of the Sierra Club residing in New Orleans at the time. Interview with Doris Falkenheiner, former board member, Delta Chapter of the Sierra Club, June 31, 2009; Ms. Falkenheiner recorded the sales agent at Jones Island.

p. 27 has more buffalo fish . . . : U.S. Fish and Wildlife Service, "The Atchafalaya, America's Greatest River Swamp," 1978, p. 7, states, "The aquatic resources of the floodway are phenomenal . . . over 85 fish species occur in the floodway, and their populations frequently exceed 1,000 pounds per acre."

p. 27 will siphon half of . . . : "Final Environmental Impact Statement," p. 22.

p. 27 under heavy pressure to . . . : Reuss, pp. 249–64, describing early controversy on Corps plans.

p. 27 It took time to . . . : Ibid., pp. 273–53, describing later controversy, negotiations, and new Atchafalaya Floodway plan.

Expressway

p. 29 After a five count . . . : Personal interview with Bill Borah, February 2009. For a full description of the freeway and its antecedents and politics, see Richard F. Weingroff, "The Battles of New Orleans–Vieux Carré Riverfront Expressway (I-310)," http://www.fhwa.dot.gov/infrastructure/neworleans.cfm.

p. 29 A spur of Interstate 10 . . . : Jonathan Mark Souther, *New Orleans on Parade* (Baton Rouge: Louisiana State University Press, 2006), p. 65.

p. 30 It was the . . . : Kelman, *A River*, p. 197.

p. 30 Recent law graduates, they . . . : Borah interview.

p. 30 It started with a . . . : Kelman, *A River*, pp. 206–7.

p. 30 Like many individuals who . . . : Richard Baumbach and William E. Borah, *The Second Battle of New Orleans: A History of the Vieux Carré Riverfront Expressway Controversy* (Tuscaloosa: University of Alabama Press), 1981.

p. 30 For the previous one . . . : Alexander Garvin, *The American City* (New York: McGraw-Hill, 2002), p. 474.

p. 31 In 1962, just as . . . : Kelman, *A River*, p. 201.

p. 31 Putting the expressway down in . . . : "The Battles of New Orleans—Vieux Carré Riverfront Expressway," http://fhwa.dot.gov/infrastructure/neworleans.cfm.

p. 31 At the same time . . . : Raymond A. Mohl, in John Bauman et al., *From Tenements to Taylor Homes* (University Park: Pennsylvania State University, 2000), p. 238.

p. 31 The highway bureau . . . : Walker Percy, *Signposts in a Strange Land*, edited by Patrick Samway (New York: Farrar, Straus, and Giroux), 1991, p. 16.

p. 31 The final option was . . . : Garvin, p. 474.

p. 31 In his last few . . . : "The Battles of New Orleans—Vieux Carré Riverfront Expressway," http://fhwa.dot.gov/infrastructure/neworleans.cfm.

p. 32 A few months later . . . : Mohl, p. 237.

p. 32 "the magnolia curtain" . . . : Kelman, *A River*, p. 210.

p. 32 Another factor was the . . . : Garvin, p. 474.

p. 32 A lawsuit generated by . . . : Souther, pp. 70–71.

p. 32 Then came another act . . . : Borah interview. The description of the Hannan meeting and its aftermath is taken from this interview and a subsequent interview with Archbishop Philip Hannan, April 2009.

p. 34 Instead of agreeing he . . . : Conversation with Jerome Glazer, spring 1984.

Elvis

p. 36 The pelicans are back . . . : R. H. Chabreck, *Coastal Marshes* (Minneapolis: University of Minnesota Press, 1988, pp. 93–94.

p. 36 It was the signature . . . : James Tanner, "Original Distribution," *The Ivory-Billed Woodpecker* (National Audubon Society, 1942), p. 3.

p. 36 The Pearl runs down . . . : United States Geological Survey, http://ms.water.usgs.gov/ms_proj/eric/pearl.html.

p. 36 intensely wild by nature . . . : Tim Gallagher, *The Grail Bird: Hot on the Trail of the Ivory-Billed Woodpecker* (Boston: Houghton Mifflin, 2005), p. 6.

p. 37 The ivory bill lived in . . . : Jerome A. Jackson, *In Search of the Ivory-Billed Woodpecker* (New York: HarperCollins, 2004), p. 22.

p. 37 The last ivory-bill families . . . : Ibid., p. 150.

p. 37 One of the last . . . : The following paragraph as described in George Lowery, Jr., *Louisiana Birds* (Baton Rouge: Louisiana State University Press), 1960, p. 416.

p. 37 They got some grainy . . . : Ibid.

p. 37 The call on the disk . . . : Jackson, *In Search*, p. 17.

p. 37 By the 1950s Lowery . . . : The following paragraph as described in Gallagher, p. 9.

p. 37 More than a decade . . . : The following paragraph as described in ibid., p. 21.

p. 38 In the 1990s a . . . : "Profiles of Birds: Historic Ranges and 21 Reported Sightings of Ivory-billed Woodpeckers since 1944," http://www.birdersworld .com/brd/default.aspx?c=a&id=471.

p. 38 The hunter was a . . . : "Elusive Ivory-billed Woodpecker Not Extinct After All: LSU Played "Integral Role" in Discovery; LSE Experts Available to the Media," http://www.lsu.com/UNV002.NSF/(NoteID)/1845D3A64A34D12786256FF1 0076459C?OpenDocument.

p. 38 He described characteristics of . . . : Gallagher, p. 25.

p. 38 Nikkon funded a search . . . : "Elusive Ivory-billed Woodpecker."

Low Water

p. 46 This urban green . . . : Phase 1, U.S. Army Corps of Engineers, vol. 1, November 2004, pp. 114–25; see also Kelman, *A River*, pp. 155–56, and L. Ronald Forman and Joseph Logsden, *Audubon Park: An Urban Eden* (New Orleans: Friends of the Zoo, 1985), pp. 85, 141. The descriptions of early Audubon Park that follow are taken from this source.

p. 46 He designed a commons . . . : Phase 1, p. 119, fig. 54 (depicting Olmstead's original design, and extended open space circled by pedestrian walkways).

p. 46 The city wasted little . . . : Ibid., pp. 118–21.

p. 46 park lay Camp Louis . . . : Ibid., p. 62. The description of Camp Louis and the buffalo soldiers that follows is taken from this source. For more on the buffalo soldiers, see Brenna Farrell, "The Buffalo Soldiers: Forgotten Heroes of the West," available at http://home.inreach.com/kfarrell/buffalosoldiers.html.

p. 47 Black cavalry . . . : Ibid., p. 71.

p. 47 "brass letters" . . . : Ibid.

p. 47 hear Mahalia Jackson singing . . . : Ibid., pp. 107–12. The description of Mahalia Jackson that follows is taken from this source. For more on Mahalia Jackson in New Orleans, see Jules Victor Schwerin, *Got To Tell It*, available at http://books .google.com/books?id=MGQSAAAACAAJ&dq=mahalia+jackson.

p. 47 let it decay beyond repair . . . : Liz Scott Monaghan, "Splashing in the Audubon Natatorium," *New Orleans Magazine*, June 2002, available at http:// www.joecarvajal.com/AudubonParkPoolNarrative.html. The pool was finally demolished and, over considerable resistance from the park's neighbors, replaced by a smaller version with constricted hours of use.

p. 47 She later recalled that . . . : Phase 1, p. 107. The description of the Jackson house, Pension Town, and Pinching Town that follows is taken from this source.

p. 48 the Bisso family which . . . : Ibid., p. 102.

p. 48 nineteen vessels along the . . . : Ibid., p. 6.

p. 48 Ames Crevasse . . . : Ibid., p. 91.

p. 48 Whether the Corps can . . . : See Oliver A. Houck, "Can We Save New Orleans?" *Tulane Environmental Law Journal*, 2006, vol. 19, no. 1, (describing local Corps history, politics, prospects).

p. 49 The Marsalis motel in Shrewsbury . . . : Interview with Ellis Marsalis, Sr., by Lawrence N. Powell, September 15, 1988. The description of the Marsalis guests is taken from this interview.

p. 50 "scramble like animals" . . . : Carter, *Lower Mississippi*, p. 233.

p. 50 "Grub pile!" . . . : Ibid.

Parish Line

p. 52 "ponds, sinkholes, and limbs" . . . : Email from Levee Board, March 1, 2007, posted at http://www.lenny-jaeger.com/Batture.html.

p. 52 started barricading roads that . . . : Bill Walsh and Stephanie Grace, *Times-Picayune*, "Jefferson Parish Sheriff Harry Lee Dies," October 1, 2007, available at http://blog.nola.com/times-picayune/2007/10/jefferson_parish_sheriff_harry_1.html.

p. 53 "rinky dink automobiles" . . . : Ibid.

Southport

p. 56 the Duchess of Windsor . . . : Adela Rogers St. Johns, "Windsor Drinks Only Casually," *New Orleans Item*, November 27, 1940, p. 1.

p. 56 "Death Calls the Turn" . . . : Ken Gormin, "Death Calls the Turn on Rudy O'Dwyer, One of Fabulous Figures," *New Orleans Item*, November 27, 1940, p. 1. All information in the paragraph is taken from this article.

p. 56 "Colorful Figure Dies" . . . : Ibid.

p. 56 "fastest cabin cruiser in" . . . : Ibid.

p. 56 his aviary of three thousand . . . : Ibid.

p. 57 The Original Southport was . . . : "4 More Indicted in Louisiana," *New York Times*, February 14, 1936.

p. 57 Marcello family of the . . . : John H. Davis, *Mafia Kingfish: Carlos Marcello and the Assassination of John F. Kennedy*, (New York: McGraw-Hill, 1989), pp. 29, 134.

p. 57 French Creoles were so addicted . . . : Herbert Asbury, *The French Quarter: An Informal History of the New Orleans Underworld* (New York: Basic Books, 2008), p. 213.

p. 57 In the 1890s, the . . . : Thomas L. Jones, "Carlos Marcello: Big Daddy in the Big Easy, Coming to America," Crime Library, last accessed June 19, 2009, http://www.trutv.com/library/crime/gangsters_outlaws/family_epics/marcello/2.html.

p. 57 Hennessy was gunned down : . . . : Ibid. See also Carter, *Lower Mississippi*, pp. 312–21.

p. 58 made target practice on . . . : Ibid.

p. 58 Joe Hyland moved operations . . . : Kevin Kolb, "The New Southport Hall, Upcoming Events & Things To Do," last accessed June 19, 2009, http://upcoming.yahoo.com/venue/132464/.

p. 58 Hyland brought in two . . . : Ibid.

p. 58 the New Forest Club . . . : Blake Pontchartrain, "New Orleans Know It All," *Gambit Weekly*, November 11, 2003, last accessed June 19, 2009, http://bestofneworleans.com/gyrobase/Content?oid=oid%3A31151.

p. 58 O'Dwyers had won the . . . : Ibid.

p. 58 As Rudy's grandson recently . . . : Interview with Ashton O'Dwyer, January 2008.

p. 58 form of Carlos Marcello . . . : Jones.

p. 58 "Drive the bums out" . . . : Ibid.

p. 59 least a thousand machines . . . : Davis, pp. 31–33.

p. 59 more upscale Beverly Club . . . : Ibid., p. 40.

p. 59 The New Orleans FBI . . . : Ibid., p. 34.

p. 59 Free Parish of Jefferson . . . : "Stops Louisiana Betting," *New York Times*, January 24, 1909.

p. 59 Kefauver held public hearings . . . : Davis, pp. 56–61.

p. 59 a record 152 times . . . : Ibid., p. 57.

p. 59 "I wouldn't know" . . . : Ibid.

p. 59 another new club, O'Dwyer's . . . : Blake Pontchartrain.

p. 60 ten thousand dollars a . . . : Ibid.

p. 60 died of a heart . . . : "Jeff Raid Nets 5; George O'Dwyer Dies," *New Orleans Item*, May 27, 1953, pp. 1, 4.

p. 60 several cases against him . . . : *United States v. Marcello*, 876 F.2d 1147 (5th Cir. 1989) (overturning Marcello's conviction of violating the RICO act); *Marcello v. United States*, 196 F. 2d 437 (5th Cir. 1952) (overturning contempt conviction during Marcello's Senate committee hearings).

p. 60 and sent him to Guatamala . . . : Jones.

p. 60 Dallas in November 1963 . . . : Don Fulsom, "Carlos Marcello and the Assassination of President Kennedy," *Crime Magazine*, October 16, 2006, last accessed on June 19, 2009, http://crimemagazine.com/06/marcello, 1019–6 .htm. For a survey of evidence linking Marcello to the Kennedy assassination, see Davis, *Mafia Kingfish*.

p. 60 "in any form" . . . : The Louisiana Constitution permits "no form of gambling" and declares further that gambling shall be "suppressed by the legislature," http://senate.legis.state.la.us/documents/Constitution/constitution.pdf, Sec. 6.

p. 60 but rather in "gaming" . . . : Tyler Bridges, *Bad Bet on the Bayou* (New York: Farrar, Straus & Giroux, 2001), p. 60.

p. 60 a friend who gambled . . . : Interview with Louis Otto, January 2009.

Ghosts

p. 66 They came with flashlights. "Gone Are the Days," *News-Examiner* (Gallatin, Tenn.), May 10, 1979, p. 5. The details of the destruction of Welham plantation that follow are taken from this source.

p. 66 Granted, they owned the . . . : Bill Grady, "Plantation's Demolition Shocks Hester Area Residents," *Times-Picayune*, May 4, 1979, p. 1. The details that follow concerning efforts to guard the plantation from destruction are taken from this source.

p. 66 "We can't respond to" . . . : "Plantation Home Bulldozed; Oil Firm Says Saving One Is Enough," *Houston Chronicle*, May 6, 1979, § 4, p. 5.

p. 66 "The Rape of Welham" . . . : "The Rape of Welham," *Times-Picayune*, May 8, 1979, § 1, p. 12.

p. 66 Cartoons showed Marathon Oil . . . : "Reversed Masthead and Banner Cartoon," *News-Examiner* (Lutcher, LA), May 10, 1979, § 1, p. 4.

p. 67 "sordid," "dastardly" . . . "to do" . . . : Fen Montaigne, "House Denounces Plantation Destruction," *States-Item* Bureau.

p. 67 "from Ohio, New Jersey" . . . : Ibid.

p. 67 "figured they'd do this" . . . : Grady, p. 1. The sentence following regarding the commencement of the destruction is also from this source.

p. 67 "great sugar plantation dwellings" . . . : The River Road, http://www.nps.gov/ history/NR/travel/louisiana/riverroad.htm, last accessed August 18, 2008.

p. 67 there were 5,000 slaves . . . : John McQuaid, "Transforming the Land," *Times-Picayune*, May 21, 2000, http://www.nola.com/speced/unwelcome/index .ssf?/speced/unwelcome/stories/0521transforming.html. The other figures documenting the number of slaves in the region are also from this source.

p. 68 the plantations started to . . . : Mary Gehman, "Touring Louisiana's Great River Road," Introduction Section, http://www.margaretmedia.com/river_road/intro .htm; McQuaid. The description of the fall of the great plantations and changes in communities that follows is taken from these two sources.

p. 68 136 major facilities in . . . : Greenpeace, *We All Live Downstream: The Mississippi River and the Natural Toxics Crisis* (1989), p. 91.

p. 68 The owners were even . . . : McQuaid; Barbara Allen, "Cradle of a Revolution: The Industrial Transformation of Louisiana's Lower Mississippi River," *Technology & Culture*, January 2006, vol. 47, no. 1. The description of the effects of industrial development on rural towns is also taken from this source.

p. 68 Louisiana's understanding with the . . . : John Maginnis, *The Last Hayride* (Baton Rouge: Darkhorse Press, 1984), pp. 5–7. "Huey [P. Long] set the standard for his successors to govern by: a massive, centralized government powered by oil, a wealth-sharing plan for politicians and cronies and high political theater for the people [with low personal taxes]. . . . The middle class, in effect, has been bought off."

p. 69 the legislature exempted industry . . . : Oliver A. Houck, "This Side of Heresy: Conditioning Louisiana's Ten-Year Industrial Tax Exemption upon Compliance with Environmental Laws," 61 *Tulane Law Review* 289, 295, pp. 03–04 (1986).

p. 69 The owner of Laura . . . : John DeSantis, "Laura Plantation Rises from the Ashes," *Houma Courier* (Houma, LA), August 7, 2006, http://www.houmatoday .com/apps/pbcs.dll/article?AID=/20060807/NEWS/608070311/1025/newson.

Rivermen

p. 70 half horse and half . . . : Carter, *Lower Mississippi*, p. 216 (quoting stanza of "The Hunters of Kentucky": "no matter what the force is / we'll show him that Kentucky boys are / alligator horses.")

p. 71 nearly five hundred flatboats . . . : Ibid. In their heyday, from 1820 to 1830, the flatboat numbers rose to three thousand a year.

p. 71 "inhospitable and impenetrable wilderness" . . . : Ibid., pp. 125–26, quoting Andrew Elliot, who was commissioned by the United States government in 1796 to explore the country's western boundaries along the Ohio and Mississippi rivers.

p. 71 "But to swim this" . . . : John G. Neihardt, *The River and I* (Albany: State University of New York Press, 2008), p. 3.

p. 71 a misdeed in Memphis. Carter, p. 176.

p. 72 "half-alligator" . . . "ride tornaders" . . . : Bob Dyer, "Mike Fink," Songwright Pub. Inc. Mark Twain's classic account of rivermen bravado begins: "Whoo-oop! I'm the original iron-jawed, brass-mounted, copper-bellied corpse-maker from the wilds of Arkansaw!—Look at me! I'm the man they call Sudden Death and General Desolation. Sired by a hurricane, dam'd by an earthquake, half-brother to the cholera, nearly related to the small-pox on my mother's side! Look at me! I'll take nineteen alligators and a bar'l of whiskey for breakfast when I'm in robust health, and a bushel of rattlesnakes and a dead body when I'm ailing!" Mark Twain, *Life on the Mississippi*, p. 18. Who even makes up things in like terms today?

p. 72 a habit of shooting . . . : Henry Howe, "Historical Collections of Ohio," interview with Capt. John Fink (a purported relative of Mike Fink), available at http://encyclopedia.stateuniversity.com/pages/15135/Mike-Fink.html.

p. 72 picked off the warlock . . . : B. A. Botkin, "Heroes and Boasters," *The American People: Stories, Legends, Tales, Traditions, and Songs* (New Brunswick, NJ: Transaction Publishers, 1998), p. 32.

p. 72 Fink was brought low . . . : Joseph M. Field, "Death of Mike Fink", 1847, available at http://xroads.virginia.edu/~HYPER/DETOC/SW/fink1.html.

p. 72 Dominating the New Orleans . . . : Lyle Saxon, *Gumbo Ya-Ya: A Collection of Louisiana Folk Tales* (Baton Rouge: Pelican Publishing, 2001), p. 376.

p. 72 Annie Christmas, who carried . . . : Carter, p. 175; Herbert Asbury, *The French Quarter*, pp. 82–83.

p. 72 a blond mustache that . . . : "Annie Christmas," available at http://library .thinkquest.org/J001779/anniec.htm.

p. 72 competitions among other prostitutes . . . : Asbury, p. 82.

p. 72 It was also said . . . : Saxon, p. 377.

p. 72 a necklace of beads . . . : "Annie Christmas," http://teach.clarkschools.net/ curriculumresources/OpenResponses/3rd_Read_OR/3_Read_Annie_ Christmas_OR.doc.

p. 72 told by Mike Fink . . . : Ibid.

p. 73 called simply the Swamp . . . : Carter, pp. 176–77; Asbury, pp. 99–105.

p. 73 House Of Rest For . . . : Asbury, pp. 101–2.

p. 73 Big Bill Sedley, the . . . : Carter, p. 175; Asbury, pp. 103–4.

p. 73 keelboats were poled north . . . : Carter, p. 216.

p. 73 were marauded by pirates . . . : Carter, pp. 171–72; Asbury, pp. 83–89.

p. 73 the Harpe brothers . . . : Carter, p. 172.

p. 73 "Mason of the Woods" . . . : Ibid.

p. 73 "Captain Plug" . . . : Ibid.; Asbury, pp. 84–85. Downriver boats were also marauded by pirates who lured them to shore or onto sandbars, took the cargoes, and left no victims alive. Asbury, pp. 85–87.

Casino

p. 78 he is on trial . . . : Mark Schleifstein, "Gov. Edwards Pleas Innocent," *Times-Picayune*, March 9, 1985, pp. A1, A4.

p. 78 "world's largest gambling casino" . . . : The name used to refer to the land-based casino Edwards was pushing for. Tyler Bridges, *Bad Bet*, p. 69.

p. 78 one-sided campaign during . . . : Edwards defeated incumbent David Treen with 62 percent of the votes and the majority in sixty-two of sixty-four parishes. Joseph G. Dawson III, *The Louisiana Governors* (Baton Rouge: Louisiana State University Press, 1990), p. 272.

p. 78 "an hour and a half" . . . : John Maginnis, *The Last Hayride*, (Baton Rouge: Gris Gris Press, 1984), p. 202.

p. 78 "with a live boy" . . . : Statement made by Edwards during the 1983 gubernatorial race, "Not Quite a Private Matter," *The Economist*, March 9, 1985, p. 30.

p. 78 greeted by a federal . . . : Mark Schleifstein, "Gov. Edwards Indicted by U.S. in Hospital Case," *Times-Picayune*, March 1, 1985, pp. A1, A4–11.

p. 79 bad memory lapses on . . . : Oliver Houck, "Why Gov. Edwards Is Pushing Hard for a Casino Here," *Times-Picayune*, March 12, 1993.

p. 79 "T-Lee" and "B-True" . . . : Bridges, *Bad Bet*, p. 36.

p. 79 "revitalize" the state's economy. *Times-Picayune*, December 19, 1985, p. 1.

p. 79 "Do you know what" . . . : Interview with Edwin Edwards, spring 1983.

p. 79 "The man *paid* the" . . . : Ibid.

p. 79 "the messiah," laid out . . . : Conversation with Edmund Reggie, spring 1983. Judge Reggie, also from Crowley, Louisiana, was a major backer of Governor Edwards.

p. 79 There would be only . . . : The final casino bill in fact called for only one land-based casino. Act 384: House Bill No. 2010, The Louisiana Economic Development and Gaming Corporation Law, Acts of State of Louisiana, Volume I, June 18, 1992 (substitute for House Bill No. 1651), p. 1146.

p. 80 "an all-Louisiana enterprise" . . . : Reggie interview.

p. 80 Rayne, the Frog Capitol . . . : City of Rayne, rayne.org, last accessed on June 17, 2009.

p. 80 "they did . . . natives" . . . : Heard by the author on WWL Talk Radio in New Orleans, 1986.

p. 80 a free trip to . . . : Tyler Bridges, "Developer Flew N.O. Officials to Hawaii," *Times-Picayune*, April 16, 1992, A8.

p. 80 "You would . . . on islands . . . has deceased also" . . . : Oliver A. Houck, "Letter from New Orleans," unpublished manuscript, July 1993. Remarks of Louisiana Senator John Hainkel (on file with author).

p. 80 single land-based casino . . . : Bridges, *Bad Bet*, pp. 58–69.

p. 81 "chaos" with members . . . : Ed Anderson and Peter Nicholas, "House Approves Casino Bill," *Times-Picayune*, June 9, 1992, p. A8.

p. 81 "literally jumping from their" . . . : Rep. David Vitter, "The Political Corruption of Gambling Has Begun," *Times-Picayune*, June 11, 1992, p. B6.

p. 81 "bad football play gone" . . . : Ibid.

p. 81 "Gee Toto, I don't" . . . : Bruce Eggler, "Casino Watch," *Times-Picayune*, June 13, 1992 (quoting state Rep. Charlie Riddle, D-Marksville).

p. 81 Ten major casino companies . . . : Tyler Bridges, "The Winner," *Times-Picayune*, November 6, 1992, pp. A1, A6.

p. 81 legislature had also created . . . : Ed Anderson, "Senate Panel Passes Casino Bill," *Times-Picayune*, June 11, 1992, pp. A1, A8.

p. 81 consortium of local businessmen . . . : Frank Donze, "Harrah's Beats Long Odds to Capture Casino," *Times-Picayune*, August 12, 1993, p. A1.

p. 81 "NOW WHAT?" . . . : "NOW WHAT," *Times-Picayune*, August 12, 1993, p. A1.

p. 82 a dozen more casinos . . . : Peter Elkind, "The Big Easy's Bad Bet," *Fortune Magazine*, December 8, 1997, last accessed June 19, 2009, http://money.cnn.com/magazines/fortune/fortune_archive/1997/12/08/234913/index.htm.

p. 82 "underwater obstructions," "fast currents" . . . : Bridges, *Bad Bet*, pp. 250–51. See also James Gill, "Gambling Boats: Those Non-Moveable-on-Water Feasts," *Times-Picayune*, November 18, 1994, B9.

p. 82 "keys left in other pants" . . . : Conversation with James Gill, columnist, *Times-Picayune*, January 1994.

p. 82 the racketeering charges stuck . . . : *United States v. Edwards*, 303 F.3d 606 (5th Cir. 2002); Bridges, *Bad Bet*, p. 367.

p. 82 On one recording Edwards . . . : Mark Schleifstein, "The Government's Case," *Times-Picayune*, October 17, 1998; Christopher Baughman and William Pack, "Grand Jury Indicts Former Louisiana Governor on 28 Counts," *The Advocate Online*, November 7, 1998.

Joe Louis

p. 88 But my mind is . . . : Louisiana State Museum, "The Cabildo," available at http://lsm.crt.state.la.us/cabildo/cab8.htm.

p. 88 The traffic continued, of . . . : Judith K. Schafer, "Life and Color in Antebellum Louisiana", in Bennett H. Wall, ed., *Louisiana: A History*, 5th edition (Wheeling, IL: Harlan Davidson, 2002), p. 181.

p. 88 slaves were Jean Lafitte's . . . : Asbury, *The French Quarter*, pp. 159–63.

p. 88 The lion's share of . . . : Ibid., p. 161 ("New Orleans developed into the largest slave market in the Deep South"); Walter Johnson, *Soul by Soul: Life Inside the Antebellum Slave Market* (Cambridge: Harvard University Press, 1999), pp. 7,8 (two million slaves sent south to auction in the antebellum period, the greatest numbers to New Orleans).

p. 88 The South's ultimate nightmare . . . : Herbert Aptheker, *American Negro Slave Revolts*, pp. 249–50, available at http://books.google.com/books?id=Dp07J1rOE hcC&pg=PA90&lpg=PA90&dq=1804+natchitoches+slave+revolt&source=bl &ots=2SUkLQw18z&sig=XHowFwBLXooWFA1FwXXdYKF5_cs&hl=en&e i=yFw5StaXEIPOMpC7uIcN&sa=X&oi=book_result&ct=result&resnum=1; James H. Dormon, "The Persistent Specter: Slave Rebellion in Territorial Louisiana," *Louisiana History: The Journal of the Louisiana Historical Association*, vol. 18, no. 4, pp. 392–99, available at http://www.jstor.org/stable/4231728.

p. 88 In October 1804 Governor . . . : Ibid., p. 90; Dormon, p. 392.

p. 88 Toussaint L'Ouverture and the . . . : Junius P. Rodriguez, *Encyclopedia of Slave Resistance and Rebellion*, pp. 163–66, available at http://books.google.com/ books?id=g_kuS42BxIYC&pg=PA164&dq=rebellion+in+Saint-Domingue+to ussaint+l%27ouverture#PPA163,M1.

p. 89 "a miniature representation of" . . . : "Andry's Rebellion," October 10, 2001, available at http://everything2.com/title/Andry%2527s%2520Rebellion, footnote 1.

p. 89 A mulatto named Charles . . . : Dormon, p. 394.

p. 89 "killing poultry, cooking, drinking" . . . : Ibid., p. 395.

p. 89 As their rumor spread . . . : Ibid.

p. 90 On day two the . . . : Ibid., p. 396.

p. 90 "colors displayed and full" . . . : Ibid.

p. 90 By day three the . . . : Ibid.

p. 90 The white troops killed . . . : Ibid., p. 397.

p. 91 "Detruir le Blanc" . . . : Ibid., p. 398.

p. 91 Twenty-one of the . . . : Ibid.

p. 91 On Christmas Eve, 1811 . . . : Ibid., p. 404.

Liberty

p. 100 Tennessee Williams's brilliant metaphorical . . . : e-mail of Richard Campanella, November 21, 2008 (e-mail on file with Oliver Houck).

p. 100 "First you . . . Elysian Fields" . . . : Tennessee Williams, *A Streetcar Named Desire*, produced by Warner Bros. Pictures Inc., 1951.

p. 100 three and a half thousand . . . : Judith K. Schafer, Ph.D., "The Battle of Liberty Place: A Matter of Historic Perception," *Cultural Vistas*, Spring 1994, p. 16.

p. 100 Thirty-two people died . . . : eleven members of the militia, of whom seven were white, and twenty-one members of General Ogden's forces. Ibid.

p. 101 In 1873 a white . . . : The killings are known as the Colfax Massacre. Ted Tunnell, *Crucible of Reconstruction: War, Radicalism, and Race in Louisiana, 1862–1877* (Baton Rouge: Louisiana State University Press, 1984), pp. 190–92.

p. 101 Nearly half of them . . . : Ibid.

p. 101 six Republican officeholders to . . . : Known as the Coushatta Massacre. Ibid., pp. 199–201.

p. 101 new organization, the White . . . : William Gillett et al., *The Longest Battle, Intervention in Louisiana, The Louisiana Purchase Bicentennial Series in Louisiana History, Vol. VI, Reconstructing Louisiana* (Lafayette: Center for Louisiana Studies, University of Louisiana at Lafayette, 2001), pp. 680–81.

p. 101 "supreme danger" . . . "stupid Africanization" . . . : Adolph Reed, Jr., "The Battle of Liberty Monument—New Orleans, Louisiana White Supremacist Statue," *The Progressive*, June 1993.

p. 101 "eliminate from . . . our politics" . . . : Lawrence Powell, "A Concrete Symbol," *Southern Exposure*, Spring 1990, pp. 41–42. Quoting Chairman E. B. Kruttschnitt of New Orleans at Louisiana Constitutional Convention of 1898.

p. 102 "Africanization" than it was . . . : Schafer, p. 13. Quote of former Louisiana governor Henry Clay Warmouth.

p. 102 Ballots in those days . . . : Lisa Jane Disch, *The Tyranny of the Two-Party System*, (New York: Columbia University Press, 2002), p. 40.

p. 102 federal government claimed foul . . . : Powell, p. 40.

p. 102 a shipment of guns . . . : Schafer, p. 15.

p. 102 "For nearly two years" . . . : "Citizens of New Orleans!" *Daily Picayune*, September 13, 1874, p. 2, column 6.

p. 102 "We therefore . . . TO BE, FREE!" . . . : Ibid.

p. 102 The league drew a . . . : Schafer, pp. 15–16.

p. 102 "the Usurper and his" . . . : Alfred E. Lemon et al., *Charting Louisiana* (New Orleans: The Historic New Orleans Collection, 2003), p. 337.

p. 103 Ulysses S. Grant sent in . . . : Schafer, p. 16.

p. 103 a White League governor . . . : C. E. Richard, *Louisiana: An Illustrated History* (Baton Rouge: The Foundation for Excellence in Louisiana Broadcasting, 2003), p. 105. (Murphy Foster, a White Leaguer, took away voting rights for blacks). See also Joy J. Jackson, *New Orleans in the Gilded Age* (Baton Rouge: Louisiana State University Press, 1969), pp. 33–34, 130–31, 228–29, and Sidney James

Romero, "The Political Career of Murphy James Foster, Governor of Louisiana, 1892–1900," *Louisiana Historical Quarterly*, 28 (1946), pp. 1129–1243.

p. 103 "a mob of gentlemen" . . . : Powell, p. 41.

p. 103 Tied to the North . . . : Ibid., p. 40.

p. 103 In 1888 the site . . . : Stuart Omer Landry, *The Battle of Liberty Place: The Overthrow of Carpet-Bag Rule in New Orleans, September 14, 1874* (New Orleans: Pelican Pub. Co. 1955), p. 230.

p. 103 Three years later a . . . : Ibid.

p. 103 "usurpers" . . . "gave us our state" . . . : James W. Loewen, *Lies Across America* (New York: New Press, distributed by W. W. Norton, 1999), p. 216.

p. 103 "Governor Kellog . . . Lt. Gov. Antoine" . . . : Ibid.

p. 104 NAACP held its national . . . : Charlayne Hunter, "N.A.A.C.P. Parley Reaffirms Goals," *New York Times*, July 7, 1994, p. 25.

p. 104 "Stevie Wonder Square" . . . : Powell, p. 43.

p. 104 "Vote For The Crook" . . . : A pro–Edwin Edwards bumper sticker during his campaign for governor against KKK leader David Duke. Kent B. Germany, *New Orleans after the Promises* (Athens: University of Georgia Press, 2007), p. 27.

p. 104 finally fell through . . . : Rick Bragg, "Ex-Governor of Louisiana Gets 10 Years," *New York Times*, January 9, 2001.

p. 104 "the sentiments . . . New Orleans" . . . : Loewen, p. 217.

p. 104 FUCK OFF NAZI SCUM . . . : "Racist Liberty Place Monument," New Orleans Indy Media, June 1, 2004, http://neworleans.indymedia.org/news/2004/06/1639.php, last accessed June 19, 2009.

p. 105 a local druggist filed . . . : Reed, Jr.

p. 105 "righteous . . . . administration." : Ibid. Statement made by Louisiana attorney John Wilkinson.

p. 105 ancestor had fought with . . . : Judge Wisdom's father, Mortimer Wisdom, was a White League member who participated in the skirmish on September 14, 1874. Joel William Friedman, *Champion of Civil Rights: Judge John Minor Wisdom* (Baton Rouge: Louisiana State University Press 2009), p. 89.

p. 105 "big issue" . . . "and democracy" . . . : Statement was made by Judge John Minor Wisdom; Reed, Jr.

p. 105 Then again, Wisdom's court . . . : Friedman, p. 90.

p. 105 The state historian insisted . . . : Reed, Jr. Opinion of Jonathan Fricker, Louisiana's director of historic preservation.

p. 105 the entire platform of . . . : Powell, p. 41.

Cycling

p. 113 Originally, the path was . . . : Earl Higgins, "The Pork-Paved Bike Path," *The Delta Sierran*, 1995, http://louisiana.sierraclub.org/pdf/BikePath5%2B6_95.pdf.

p. 113 Dredging companies bought licenses . . . : Interview with Chris Gobert, June 28, 2009; Mr. Gobert represented plaintiffs in subsequent challenges to the permits.

p. 113 Their big suction pipes . . . : Herman Robinson, State of Louisiana, Department of Environmental Quality, Findings of Fact and Conclusions of Law, In the Matter of: Drave Basic Materials Inc. et al. (hereinafter DEQ Hearings).

p. 113 Within a few decades . . . : Dr. Darnell, expert testimony from DEQ Hearings.

p. 113 It took two lawsuits . . . : *Louisiana v. Lee*, 596 F.Supp. 645 (E. Dist. LA 1984) (reversed by *Louisiana v. Lee*, 758 F.2d 1081 (5th Cir. 1985); May 10, 1990, Permit Hearings with the Louisiana DEQ. A third case challenged the dredging permits under state bid laws. Gobert interview.

Homicide

p. 121 Five shootings on a . . . : Brendan McCarthy, "Violent Weekend in New Orleans Results In 5 Shot, Four Stabbed," *Times-Picayune*, July 7, 2009.

p. 121 someone killed a minister . . . : Darran Simon, "Elderly pastor and wife shot to death at their Gentilly home," *The Times-Picayune*, May 11, 2009.

p. 121 name of C-Murder . . . : Paul Purpura and C. J. Lin, "C-Murder Guilty of Second-degree Murder after Topsy-turvy Jury Action," *Times-Picayune*, August 11, 2009.

p. 122 The jury convicted . . . : The appellate court later overturned the conviction, on the grounds of inadmissable evidence, *United States v Roland W. Brown*, 490 F.2d 758 (D.C. Cir. 1973).

p. 122 We lead the nation . . . : Brendan McCarthy, "N.O. Killing Rate Leads the Nation," *Times-Picayune*, June 2, 2009.

p. 122 has protested the number . . . : Brendan McCarthy, "Police Chief Calls New Orleans Top Murder Rank Misleading," *Times-Picayune*, June 3, 2009.

p. 123 cut-purses and prostitutes . . . : Asbury, *The French Quarter* p. 4 (the women "almost without exception from the prisons and brothels of Paris"); (even the soldiers of the cast-offs of society "kidnapped, herded and shipped under guard" to Louisiana.

p. 123 "hell on earth" . . . : Ibid., p. 317.

p. 123 death by violence exceeded . . . : Historian Dennis C. Rousey, "Other than the Wild West, There Wasn't Any Place More Violent than New Orleans," *Times-Picayune*, March 30, 2009, p. A7.

p. 123 Two thirds of New Orleans . . . : Asbury, p. 316.

p. 123 "every day occurrence" . . . : Ibid., p. 315.

p. 123 "the record of one" . . . : Ibid., p. 316.

p. 123 It started with the . . . : Carter, *Lower Mississippi*; Asbury, pp. 142–53.

p. 123 "rarely a man in" . . . : Asbury, p. 145.

p. 124 dominate the metro section . . . : See p. B1, Metro Section, *Times-Picayune*, August 11, 2009, an ordinary day in New Orleans, with the headlines: Leslie Williams, "3 Wounded in Drive-by Shooting near NORD Community Center"; Gwen Filosa, "Jury Pick Starts in Quintuple Killing." The following day carried four such stories; and a month later, Ramon Antonio Vargas, "Two Die in

Especially Violent Stretch: 8 Separate Shootings Include 3-Year-Old Girl," *Times-Picayune*, September 13, 2009, p. B1.

Gypsum

p. 129 the city's only member . . . : http://www.allbusiness.com/agriculture-forestry/support-activities-agriculture/4106060–1.html. Entergy became the city's second Fortune 500 company at a later time; Freeport has since moved to Phoenix.

p. 129 Freeport owned several fertilizer . . . : Danny Kennedy, *Risky Business: The Grasberg Gold Mine*, An Independent Annual Report on P. T. Freeport Indonesia, May 1998, p. 23. The description of P. T. Freeport's operations in Louisiana and its receipt of a federal discharge permit are also taken from this source.

p. 130 Louisiana would have to . . . : Nicholas Lemann, "Hard Times in the Big Easy," *The Atlantic*, August 1987, http://www.theatlantic.com/doc/198708/big-easy.

p. 130 The one agency unhappy . . . : DEQ Response to Comments Concerning Draft Permits Proposed March 1986 for Four Phosphate Manufacturing Plants, March 1987, pp. 13–14 (on file with author).

p. 130 nineteen of their intake . . . : Water Quality Evaluation of Proposed Effluent Limits for the Four Mississippi River Phosphorus Fertilizer Plants in Louisiana, U.S. E.P.A. Region 6, Industrial Permits Division, February 25, 1986, pp. 20–21.

p. 131 an obscure requirement surfaced . . . : Evaluation and Projection of Water Quality Impacts From Nutrient Loading, December 1986, p. 42 (on file with author). The description of the ratio of phosphorus and nitrogen due to the waste discharges is also from this source.

p. 131 the state found itself . . . : Lemann.

p. 131 He purchased his critics . . . : Robert Bryce, "Spinning Gold," *Mother Jones*, September/October 1996, pp. 68–69. The description of Freeport's CEO hiring two television journalists is also taken from this source.

p. 131 He endowed separate university . . . : Oliver Houck, "Major Money's Influence in Freeport-Indonesia Affair," *Times-Picayune*, February 29, 1986, p. B7.

p. 131 provided ten million dollars . . . : Bruce Eggler, "Moffett Criticizes Environmentalists," *Times-Picayune*, December 15, 1991, p. B1, B3.

p. 131 "kick their [critics'] butts" . . . : Ibid.

p. 131 "This is . . . a religion" . . . : David E. Ortman, "All That Glitters Is Not Gold," *Mennonite Life*, September 2001, vol. 56, no. 3, last accessed at http://www.bethelks.edu/mennonitelife/2001sept/ortman.php.

p. 131 he opened the world's . . . : Bryce, p. 66.

p. 131 Freeport received insurance from . . . : Kennedy, pp. 6, 18.

p. 131 There were tales of . . . : Bryce, p. 66; Kennedy, p. 7.

p. 132 western reporters tried to . . . : Bryce, p. 67. The description of only being allowed to travel on Freeport's terms and the allowance of one *Times-Picayune* reporter visiting the mine are also from this source.

p. 132 Human rights claims stemming . . . : *Beanal v. Freeport McMoran, Inc.*, 969
F.Supp. 362, 384 (E.D. La. 1997).

p. 132 Tulane, Loyola, and UNO . . . : "Leading By Example" (advertisement),
Times-Picayune, November 16, 1995 ("The following organizations would like
to acknowledge Freeport-McMoRan as a caring corporate citizen. Through
economic development, philanthropic, environmental, education and youth
programs, it has consistently set the standard as a leader in New Orleans and the
River Region").

p. 132 pulled his headquarters out . . . : "Freeport-McMoRan's Acquires Phelps
Dodge, Becomes World's Largest Publicly-Traded Copper Company, November
20, 2006, last accessed at http://www.foxnews.com/story/0,2933,230640,00
s.html.

Fight

p. 134 They had come down . . . : Mennonite Disaster Service, Judy Martin
Godshalk, "Why People of Faith Matter after Gulf Hurricanes," September
25, 2008, available at http://mds.mennonite.net/news/articles/article/
Why_people_of_faith_matter_after_Gulf_hurricanes/browse/5/?tx_
ttnews[arc]=1&tx_ttnews[backPid]=34&tx_ttnews[pl]=2591999&tx_ttnews[p
S]=1207022400&cHash=12d83698e1.

p. 135 This was the Cannes Brulees . . . : "Kenner Historical Timeline Highlights,"
http://www.kenner.la.us/history.html.

p. 135 William Kenner came up . . . : Ibid.

p. 135 When his business partner . . . : Ibid.

p. 135 Over time, Kennertown's major . . . : Ibid., p. 2.

p. 135 The purse was two thousand . . . : Ralph Mace, "Jem Mace Champion of the
World," available at http://www.jemmace.com/JemMaceBody01.html. The
description of the fight that follows is taken largely from this source.

p. 136 "sudden eruption" . . . "and bowie knives" . . . : Ibid., p. 2, 3.

p. 137 "Tom, you are a" . . . : Boxer Rec, George Siler, "Jem Mace v. Tom Allen,"
available at http://www.boxrec.com/media/index.php/Jem_Mace_vs._Tom_
Allen.

p. 137 boxing, which has lost . . . : CBS Sports, Gregg Doyel, "Boxing's Big Hurrah?
More like Last Gasp Before MMA Seizes Day," May 3, 2007, available at http://
www.cbssports.com/columns/story/10164182.

Gustav

p. 140 Notwithstanding, the director of . . . : Matthew Pleasant and Robert Zullo,
"As Parish Flooded, Emergency Director Was at an LSU Game," *Houma Courier*,
September 17, 2008.

IT

p. 147 "Honey, they're going to" . . . : Interview by Claire Yancey, Tulane University
law student, with Al and Theresa Róbert and Al Róbert, Jr., October 23, 2008
(hereinafter Róbert interview). The description of the conversation between
Teresa Róbert and Ruby Cointment is also from this source.

p. 148 an old slave quarters . . . : Ibid.

p. 148 But here was Governor . . . : Dorothy Mahan, "People Power: Two
Homemakers Win Landmark Environmental Decision," *Preservation in Print*,
December 1992, p. 16. The description "world's largest waste disposal site" is also
from this source.

p. 148 In the 1970s, much . . . : Interview by Claire Yancey, Tulane University law
student, with Willie Fontenot, September 21, 2008 (hereinafter Fontenot
interview). Mr. Fontenot formerly served as community liaison officer for the
office of the Louisiana Attorney General. The details of the death of Curly
Jackson are also from this source.

p. 148 "you can't make an" . . . : Oral interview with Willie Fontenot, April 2008. See
also Houck, "This Side of Heresy," pp. 323–29, describing the volume and effects
of hazardous waste disposal in Louisiana.

p. 148 a Louisiana official ran . . . : Al Róbert, Jr., "The IT Decision: An Evaluation of
Its Factual, Judicial, and Legislative History and a Consideration of Its Future,"
The Louisiana Environmental Lawyer, Summer 2004, vol. 8, no. 1, p. 2. The details
of the site selection and land purchase are also from this source.

p. 149 The IT project called for . . . : Róbert interview.

p. 149 "because we know if" . . . : Mahan, p. 16.

p. 149 and began collecting signatures . . . : Róbert interview. The description of
citizens calling to remove their names and local businesses boycotting the
restaurant is also from this source.

p. 149 At one point IT . . . : Fontenot interview.

p. 149 IT offered to fly . . . : Róbert interview. The description of IT's California
facility is also from this source.

p. 150 The waste site flooded . . . : Ibid.

p. 150 It was also on top . . . : Al Róbert, Jr., "The IT Decision," p. 4.

p. 150 The state approved the . . . : Ibid., p. 3.

p. 150 "never met an industry" . . . : Ibid., p. 14, n. 152, stating the proposition as "as
maxim" in Louisiana.

p. 150 The trial court, plainly . . . : Interview by Claire Yancey, Tulane University
law student, with Steve Irving, November 21, 2008. Mr. Irving represented the
Róberts before the state environmental agencies and the courts.

p. 150 Undaunted, the Róberts soldiered . . . : *Save Ourselves, Inc. v. Louisiana Envtl.
Control Comm'n*, 452 So.2d 1152, 1155–61, 1984. The holding that the state must examine all reasonable alternatives before making a decision is also from this source.

p. 151 They denied the IT . . . : Mahan, p. 16–17.

p. 151 The IT site is now . . . : Fontenot interview.

Squatters

p. 156 "bad girls" up here . . . : Oldie King, "Lawd Lawd." Response to "I wanna hear . . . ," August 24, 2007, http://www.network54.com/Forum/259029/message/1187989873/Lawd+Lawd.

p. 156 "wretched little log cabins" . . . : Mark Twain, *Life on the Mississippi* (New York: Harper & Brothers, 1901), p. 82.

p. 157 "one or two jeans-clad" . . . : Ibid.

p. 157 Its job was to . . . : J. P. Kemper, *Rebellious River* (Boston: Humphries, 1949), pp. 59–60 (1972); Reuss, pp. 14–47.

p. 157 It took a series . . . : Joseph I. Arnold, *The Evolution of the Flood Control Act of 1936*, Office of History, U.S. Army Corps of Engineers, 1988.

p. 157 flood stages kept on . . . : Corps levee and drainage projects have been largely responsible for a constantly rising flood line on the Mississippi River. The Corps was forced to recalculate the line as early as 1964. See H.R. Doc, No. 308, 89th Congress, 2d. see Session (1964). See also C. S. Belt in "1973 Flood and Man's Constriction of the Mississippi River," 189 *Science* 681 (1975), concluding that the 1973 flood's record was manmade.

p. 157 The Carrollton area was . . . : R. Christopher Goodwin and Associates, "Phase I Cultural Resource Survey and Archeological Inventory of the Proposed Carrollton Revetment Project, Orleans Parish, Louisiana, Vol. I, Nov. 2004." The description of the railroad station, Carrollton Hotel and Gardens, and Southport landing are taken from this source.

p. 157 *East Lynne*, a popular . . . : Personal interview with Louis Otto, January 2009, a Carrollton resident who attended the performances as a boy.

p. 158 begun to boom . . . : Thomas Sancton, "Batture Camp Life Doomed," *New Orleans Item*, December 16, 1952, p. 1, col. 3. ("The settlement goes back to the city's founding. But its growth in New Orleans Parish limits came during the Depression. Houses were built for cost of nails—a few dollars.") Called the "Depression Colony," it was described as a "ramshackle community of cottages and shacks." See Slyoldawg, "Found This Info and Link," response to Batture Dwellers, August 25, 2007, at http://www.network54.com/Forum/259029/message/1188095538/.

p. 158 Some made their living . . . : John Paul Bordes, "Waiting on the Levee," *John-Paul Sez: Carrollton and New Orleans, Columns from The Town of Carrollton News* (New Orleans: Goodey Sales Promotions, 1978), p. 28. See also personal interview with Connie, January 2009, who fished and gathered firewood in his skiff from the Carrollton batture in the 1930s.

p. 158 of the street vendors . . . : Bordes, "The Old Carrollton Market," ibid., p. 7; "Street Sounds," ibid., p. 32.

p. 158 jumping barefoot from trunk . . . : Interview with Louis Otto.

p. 158 Captain Bisso, the maritime . . . : Jim Sharp, "Engineers Still Pet Peeve of a Aged Batture Man Facing Loss of Home," *New Orleans States Item*, October 27, 1948, p. 12.

p. 158 Noah's Ark Baptist Church . . . : Ibid.

p. 158 Newspaper headlines tell the . . . : "Deadline to Quit Batture Is Fixed," *Times-Picayune*, December 16, 1952, p. 19, col. 1; "River Folks Are Saddened by Vacate Order of Board," *Times-Picayune*, December 17, 1952, p. 22, col. 1; "Batture People to Resist Order," *Times-Picayune*, April 7, 1953, p. 5, col. 3; "Dwellers Plan Batture Battle," *Times-Picayune*, April 27, 1953, p. 9, col. 1; "Deputies Give Batture Dweller the Bad News," *Times-Picayune*, July 21, 1954, p. 5, col. 10; "Engineers Still Pet Peeve of Aged Batture Man Facing Loss of Home," *New Orleans States Item*, October 17, 1948, p. 12; Ken Wilson, "Batture Tenants Pull Out; Bulldozers Going in Today," *Times-Picayune*, July 26, 1954; "Batture Clearance Starts; Dwellers Aided in Moving," *Times-Picayune*, July 27, 1954.

p. 159 "poet laureate" of the . . . : "Poet Carried Out of Batture Home," *New Orleans Item*, July 26, 1954, p. 1, col. 2.

p. 159 cooking fires still burning . . . : J. Burton LeBlanc, "St. Gabriel and the Louisiana River Road . . . the Early Days," http://www.louisianaguru.com/. ("The women in the kitchens kept their fires burning even as mules pulled the houses resting on wooden rollers.")

p. 159 woke up to find . . . : Personal observation, January 2008.

p. 159 Ashton O'Dwyer has been . . . : Stephen Mahoney, "Landowner Suing to Remove Residents from Riverfront Property," *New Orleans City Business*, April 16, 2007; Mark Walter, "Up the River," *Times-Picayune*, May 29, 2007; personal interview with Ashton O'Dwyer, May 2008.

Oil

p. 161 multiyear survivor show . . . : For a description of this controversy and the negotiations to resolve it, see Reuss, *Designing the Bayous*, pp. 249-354.

p. 161 marvel of phantom economics . . . : See *South Louisiana Environmental Council v. Rush*, 629 F.2d 1005 (5th Cir. 1980) (finding 42 percent of project benefits illusory).

p. 161 two oil rig manufacturers . . . : The Avondale and the McDermott shipyards near Morgan City, Louisiana.

p. 162 President Carter's first acts . . . : See Marc Reisner, *Cadillac Desert: The American West and Its Disappearing Water* (New York: Viking, 1986), pp. 317–43 (describing the president's fight against submarginal water projects).

p. 162 All of south Louisiana . . . : Oliver A. Houck, "Land Loss in Coastal Louisiana: Causes, Consequences and Remedies," 58 *Tulane Law Review* 1, 1983, pp. 46–48.

p. 162 Mississippi Gulf Outlet . . . : See Dr. John Day et al, " Mister Go Must go," http://www.edf.org/documents/5665_Report%20-%20Mister%20Go%20 Must%20Go.pdf (describing the canal's destruction of over twenty thousand acres of cypress trees and its "funneling effect" in ushering Hurricanes Katrina and Rita into New Orleans and surrounding parishes.)

p. 163 additional five thousand miles . . . : National Research Council, "Drawing Louisiana's New Map: Addressing Land Loss In Coastal Louisiana," 2005, p. 30 (in fact, placing the figure higher).

p. 163 death by five thousand . . . : Estimates of the oil industry's responsibility for overall coastal land loss bottom at approximately 50 percent, with as high as 90 percent in heavily exploited areas. See, e.g., Shea Penland, Paul F. Connor Jr., and Andrew Beall, "Changes in Louisiana's Shoreline: 1855–2002," in U.S. Army Corps of Engineers, Louisiana Coastal Area, Louisiana, Ecosystem Restoration Study app. D.3 (2004), available at http://www.lca.govinearterm/ app_d/Ch_3ChangesinShoreline.pdf.; Turner, Costanza, and Scaife, "Canals and Wetland Erosion Rates in Coastal Louisiana," in Proceedings of the Conference on Coastal Erosion and Wetland Modification in Louisiana: Causes, Consequences, and Options 73 (U.S. Fish & Wildlife Service, D. Boesch ed. 1982), ("In general, where canal density is high, land losses are high; where land losses are low, canal density are low. Further, the land loss rates at zero canal density for all six regions [of the Louisiana Coast] average 0.091 Å 0.139% annually (meanÅstd. dev.) or about 11% of overall land loss rates from 1955 to 1978 (0.8% annually) for the whole coast. The implication is that this annual rate of 0.09% represents the combined influence of all factors except canals. Canals, therefore, may be responsible for 89% of the total land loss").

p. 163 funded by Shell Oil . . . : America's WETLAND Foundation, "Gift Detail," 2008, on file with author, showing that of $1,164,682.12 in contributions, $1,020,000.00 was made by Shell Oil; another $50,000 of this amount was provided by the American Petroleum Institute.

p. 163 thirty-six billion dollars . . . : "Exxon Mobil Tops Fortune List of Global 500," Xinhua, http://english.people.com.cn/200607/14/eng20060714 283032.html.

p. 163 four others close behind . . . : Ibid., (including Royal Dutch Shell, BP, Chevron, and Conoco Phillips).

p. 163 World of Mr. Bill, . . . : available at: http://www.mrbill.com/index.html.

p. 163 He had some video . . . : Video available at http://video.google.com/video play?docid=4694637694087008583. For subsequent Mr. Bill videos on Shell and the coast, see http://vimeo.com/6102466 and http://www.youtube.com/ watch?v=I4FUaWXKZSE.

p. 164 hustled away by the police . . . : E-mail of Han Shan, "Re: Update From Alison: Shell comes under fire at New Orleans Jazz Fest," May 4, 2009, on file with author.

p. 164 "Shell and their friends" . . . : Keith Spera, "Dr. John Backs Shell-Scolding Plane That Will Fly over Jazz Fest," *Times-Picayune*, April 10, 2009.

p. 164 A few days later . . . : Keith Spera, "Dr. John Clarifies His Position on Shell, Jazz Fest and Louisiana's Wetlands," *Times-Picayune*, April 15, 2009.

Time

p. 165 "struck with astonishment" . . . : William T. Hornaday, *Our Vanishing Wild Life* (New York: New York Zoological Society, 1913; reprinted Whitefish, MT:

Kessenger Publishing, 2008), p. 12 (quoting the ornithologist Alexander Wilson). The description of the passenger pigeon flight and mathematical calculations that follow are taken from this source.

p. 165 "It is only the pigeons" . . . : Ibid.

p. 165 "twenty or thirty dozen" . . . : Ibid.

Dog

p. 174 Louisiana's record oil spill . . . : Molly Reid, "They Got Fuel All over the Freakin' River Now," *Times-Picayune*, August 3, 2008.

p. 174 It turns out that . . . : Jen DeGregorio, "Towboat Apprentice May Have Been Asleep at the Helm," *Times-Picayune*, October 23, 2008.

p. 174 At a subsequent hearing . . . : Jen DeGregorio, "Tug's Pilot Jumped Ship to Visit Girlfriend at Time of Mississippi River Oil Spill," *Times-Picayune*, October 22, 2008. To which, a newspaper reader sent in the following comment: "This aint nothin. Hell, I fill in all the time to run this here nuke plant. Boss say he has another job he has to be at. Something about blowin. Boss say if the yella light come on, flip this here switch. If the red light come on, he say 'run Forest run!!'" posting by peepdisout, http://www.nola.com/news/index.ssf/2008/10/tugs_pilot_not_on_board_when_o.html.

Highest and Best

p. 178 "highest and best use . . . it produces" . . . : A legal concept determining land values for purposes of appraisal and taxation, which in turn incentivizes maximum development and the loss of open space. See abstract, "Highest and Best Use: The von Thunen Connection," *Appraisal Journal*, September 22, 2004, http://goliath.ecnext.com/coms2/gi_0199-3670135/Highest-and-best-use-the .html/. "The ideas of von Tunen provide a solid theoretical foundation for current definitions of highest and best use, and provide a better understanding of why the highest-valued legal and physically possible use represents the highest and best use of the land."

p. 178 the story of Papa Dukie . . . : The Subdues, "Da Music Dat Shapes Us: Papa Dukie & The Mud People," The Cacophony Society, June 30, 2007, http://thecacophonysociety.blogspot.com/2007_06_01_archive.html. The description of this group's occupation of the batture which follows is taken from this source.